MESOAMERICAN ARCHAEOLOGY
A Guide to the Literature and Other Information Sources

Guides and Bibliographies Series: 12

Mesoamerican Archaeology
A Guide to the Literature and Other Information Sources

by Susan Fortson Magee

Institute of Latin American Studies
The University of Texas at Austin

Institute of Latin American Studies
The University of Texas at Austin
William P. Glade, *Director*
Robert Malina, *Associate Director*

International Standard Book Number 0-292-75053-6
Library of Congress Catalog Card Number 81-83674

Printed by The University Printing Division of The University of Texas at Austin.
Manufactured in the United States of America.

The Guides and Bibliographies series is distributed
for the Institute of Latin American Studies by:

University of Texas Press
P. O. Box 7819
Austin, TX 78712

To Mark

Contents

Preface / ix
Introduction / 3
Related Fields / 5
  Ethnohistory / 5
  Pre-Columbian Art and Architecture / 6
Types of Sources / 7
Guides to the Literature / 7
Bibliographies / 10
  Retrospective / 10
  Current / 12
Periodicals / 14
  Directories / 14
  Journals / 17
  Indexes / 17
Abstracts / 22
Reviews / 24
Newsforms / 25
Theses and Dissertations / 27
Associations and Societies / 29
Grants and Research Centers / 31
International Agencies and Bodies / 34
Government Agencies / 35
Special Library Collections / 37
Human Relations Area Files / 39
Museums / 40
Atlases, Maps and Aerial Photographs / 42
Specialists / 45

Academic Institutions and Field Schools / 46
Biographical Dictionaries / 48
Non-Print Materials / 48
  General / 48
  Slides / 49
  Microforms / 49
Search Techniques / 49
Appendix / 55
References / 63
Additional References / 65
Index / 67

Preface

This guide is the culmination of a project undertaken for a graduate level course dealing with reference sources in the social sciences. It is intended for use by students whose interests are in Mesoamerican archaeology; it may also be of value as a reference tool for librarians. Each source listed in this guide is given a numerical accession symbol. When necessary, reference is then made to this number so that users may locate the source readily.

Throughout the compilation of this guide, the writer sought out as much expert advice and input as possible. Sincere gratitude and appreciation go to Professors James Neely, Jeremiah Epstein, and Richard Schaedel, all of the Department of Anthropology at The University of Texas at Austin. Also, thanks go to Dr. Agnes Reagan, of The University of Texas Graduate School of Library and Information Science, for it was her idea to set the writer out on this ambitious undertaking.

MESOAMERICAN ARCHAEOLOGY
A Guide to the Literature and Other Information Sources

INTRODUCTION

Mesoamerican archaeology is concerned with documenting the cultural history and cultural processes of a particular area of the New World prior to the arrival of the Spanish in 1519. The geographic boundaries of Mesoamerica are dictated by Paul Kirchoff's enumeration of traits that were shared by otherwise diverse cultures. Kirchoff's list[1] includes such diagnostics as:

Agricultural calendar of 365 days
Ball courts
Cacao used as medium of exchange
Codices
Cotton armor
Hieroglyphic writing
Human sacrifice on a large scale
Pantheon that includes a Feathered Serpent rain god and culture hero
Ritual use of paper, rubber, and the number 13

With these criteria, the northern boundary of Mesoamerica is an uneven line drawn between the Sinaloa and Pánuco rivers in what is now northern Mexico. The southern boundary extends from the mouth of the Ulúa River in Honduras to the Nicoya Peninsula of Costa Rica.

In this region, a number of ancient civilizations arose and went through periods of expansion and contraction. For example, Helfritz reminds us that in Mexico alone, at least 11,000 archaeological sites have been recorded by the Instituto Nacional de Antropología e Historia (INAH). Of these, more than 3,000 are at least of medium size, but fewer than 10 percent of the 3,000 have been archaeologically investigated.[2]

Information on Mesoamerican archaeology is scattered in monograph series, articles, and conference papers. However, an overview of the subject, and perhaps the best introduction to the archaeology of Mesoamerica, is given in Weaver's *The Aztecs, Maya, and Their Predecessors.* The author traces the culture history of Mesoamerica and devotes a chapter to culture processes, problems, and trends. Weaver's interest in newcomers to the field shines through, for she provides a glossary of selected deities and of terminology frequently encountered in Mesoamerican archaeology. A fourteen-page bibliography is also included.

Robert Wauchope's sixteen-volume *Handbook of Middle American Indians* is undoubtedly the most comprehensive work dealing with Mesoamerican archaeology ever to be published. The *Handbook* covers all bases, devoting sea separate volumes to ethnology, physical anthropology, linguistics, archaeology, ethnohistory, and the natural environment. Of special importance to students of Mesoamerican archaeology are volumes 2 and 3, *Archaeology of Southern Mesoamerica,* and volumes 10 and 11, *Archaeology of Northern Mesoamerica.* Articles contained in these volumes are long and scholarly, and many illustrations are provided. Researchers should also check other volumes in the set for pertinent information. At the end of each volume there is a subject index and a bibliography of the references cited. No subject index yet exists for the entire set; however, volume 16, *Sources Cited and Artifacts Illustrated,* serves as a bibliographic guide to researchers. This volume also provides provenience information for the artifacts illustrated in each of the *Handbook* volumes.

Other useful introductory sources include Willey's *An Introduction to American Archaeology, Volume One: North and Middle America,* and Sanders and Price's *Mesoamerica: The Evolution of a Civilization.* Two recent publications in this area are Richard E. W. Adams's *Prehistoric Mesoamerica* (1977), and Norman Hammond's *Mesoamerican Archaeology: New Approaches,* a collection of papers presented by leading scholars at a 1972 symposium on Mesoamerican archaeology.

For various historical, political, and geographical reasons, archaeological documentation of Mesoamerican populations is weighted heavily toward those civilizations that developed in Mexico and Guatemala: the Olmecs, Totonacs, Zapotecs, Mixtecs, Aztecs, Toltecs, and Mayas. Much less is known about ancient peoples outside of Mexico and Guatemala, but recent research efforts have sought to remedy this.

This guide is an attempt to give the user a *sample* of the types of literature and other information sources that exist for this field. Its purpose is twofold: to update Wauchope's *Handbook of Middle American Indians* and to provide a means of access to information that is not covered in the *Handbook.* An attempt has been made to achieve a balance between English and foreign language materials and, where applicable, between current (i.e., post-1965, an arbitrarily chosen date) and retrospective sources. Users of this guide should keep in mind the dangers inherent in the ethnocentric assumption that all really important material will have been translated into English. Such an assumption has no place in the profession, and, as this guide helps to show, much literature does exist in foreign publications that is never translated into English.

Archaeology, by its very nature, demands a multi- or interdisciplinary approach to meeting its objectives. Archaeologists must draw from such scattered disciplines as botany, physics, geography, geology, zoology, art, chemistry, and history. In addition, archaeologists must remain in close contact with colleagues in other branches of anthropology. This guide stands as an attempt to bring order out of chaos. The materials included were selected either because they relate directly to Mesoamerican archaeology or because they provide access points for a multidisciplinary approach to the subject.

To locate materials on Mesoamerican archaeology, researchers will wish to consult the card catalog as well as a variety of other sources. The Library of Congress (LC) and Sears subject headings drawn up to cover this topic include:

INDIANS OF MEXICO–ANTIQUITIES
INDIANS OF CENTRAL AMERICA–ANTIQUITIES
EXCAVATIONS (ARCHAEOLOGY)–[Name of Country]
[Name of region]
country –ANTIQUITIES
city
[or ethnic group]
[Site name] SITE, [Country] (e.g., LA VENTA SITE, MEXICO)

It also is possible to locate materials by looking up any of the corporate names referred to throughout this guide to obtain lists of their publications contained in the library.

Shelf browsing may be done by going to Library of Congress sections F 1219-1221; F 1434-1435.3 (see Appendix) and to Dewey sections 913.72; 917.2; 972.01; 709.72.

RELATED FIELDS

The goals of archaeology are met not only by fieldwork at a site but also by the study of ethnographic differences. In their search for explanations, archaeologists do not overlook sources of information from related fields. Primary among these are ethnohistory and pre–Columbian art and architecture.

Ethnohistory

A number of important works dating from the periods prior to, during, and immediately after the Conquest have survived. Archaeological ethnohistory concerns itself with using these historical informants to help reconstruct the archaeological past.

For example, archaeologists are fortunate to have native Indian documents such as the *Books of Chilam Balam*[3] for the Yucatán area and the *Popol Vuh*[4] for the highland Maya area. In addition, eyewitness accounts by Spanish conquistadors such as Bernal Díaz del Castillo[5] and the Anonymous Conqueror[6] provide researchers with chronicles of Middle American Indian life at the time of contact. Following the Conquest, the writings of missionaries supply additional primary source materials on ancient customs, traditions, and legends. Several outstanding works were written during this period. Chief among these is Fray Bernardino de Sahagún's *The General History of the Things of New Spain: Florentine Codex,* which is based on interviews with Aztec elders. Other important works were written by Durán[7] and by Las Casas.[8] Bishop Fray Diego de Landa's *Relación de las Cosas de Yucatán* stands as a landmark for its recording of Maya life. For detailed information on how to retrieve ethnohistorical information, the best source is the *Handbook of Middle American Indians,* volumes 12-15, *Guide to Ethnohistorical Sources,* by Howard F. Cline. More general information is found in Griffin (3) and the *Handbook of Latin American Studies* (4) in the "Guides to the Literature" section of this book, below.

Pre-Columbian Art and Architecture

In meeting their goal of tracing and explaining cultural history and cultural processes, archaeologists must not overlook the important role played by the art and architecture of a given people. Gradual changes in major and minor art as well as comparison of architectural styles are important indicators of cultural transitions.

For a ninety-page overview of pre-Columbian art, users of this guide will wish to consult the *Encyclopedia of World Art,* volume 10, *Middle American Protohistory.* Articles on the art and architecture of prehispanic Mesoamerica can also be located in various volumes of the *Handbook of Middle American Indians.* Since 1966, the Center for Pre-Columbian Studies of the Dumbarton Oaks Research Library and Collections has published a monographic series entitled "Studies in Pre-Columbian Art and Archaeology." Most recently, Aubyn Kendall has compiled a bibliography entitled *The Art and Archaeology of Pre-Columbian Middle America: An Annotated Bibliography of Works in English.*

Three outstanding works that discuss and/or provide photographs of archaeological ruins in Mesoamerica are Marquina's *Arquitectura Prehispánica,* Rickards's *The Ruins of Mexico,* and Maudslay's *Archaeology.* Stephens's *Incidents of Travel in Central America, Chiapas, and Yucatán* is invaluable for its line drawings of Mesoamerican ruins, stelae, and sculpture.

For current publications in American and foreign art periodicals and museum bulletins, consult the *Art Index*;[9] use standard LC subject headings and investigate all *See also* references. Another source for current international literature published in periodicals and books in the *Bulletin Signalétique* (33).

To locate works listed in the card catalog, the following LC and Sears subject headings should be used:

INDIANS OF MEXICO–ART
INDIANS OF MEXICO–ARCHITECTURE
INDIANS OF CENTRAL AMERICA–ART
INDIANS OF CENTRAL AMERICA–ARCHITECTURE

Shelf browsing may be done in the Dewey section 709.72 and the Library of Congress sections F 1219.3A6; F 1219.3A7; F 1434.2A.

TYPES OF SOURCES

Information on Mesoamerican archaeology can be located in many types of sources. These include: guides to the literature; bibliographies; periodicals; abstracts and reviews; newspapers and newsletters; theses and dissertations; the publications of societies, associations, research centers, international organizations, government agencies, libraries housing special collections, museums, and academic institutions; atlases and maps; and nonprint materials.

Depending on a researcher's interest, different types of materials covered in this guide will carry different weights. This guide attempts to provide a sampling of the types of sources that are of value; the user of this guide is then free to choose those types that are most applicable.

GUIDES TO THE LITERATURE

Guides to the literature are important sources for acquiring an overview of any subject. In a guide one can get a feeling for the types and sources of information that are available.

No guide specific to the literature of Mesoamerican archaeology currently exists. The subject suffers because it straddles two major fields, anthropology and Latin American studies. Guides for both of these disciplines exist, but until recently there was no source that linked the two topics. Now, however, Eileen McGlynn's *Middle American Anthropology: Directory, Bibliography, and Guide to the UCLA Library Collections* serves to bridge the gap.

The works discussed in this section reflect the interdisciplinary nature of the subject and provide different access points to the literature. These are:

White, Carl M., and associates. *Sources of Information in the Social Sciences: A Guide to the Literature.* 1973.

McGlynn, Eileen. *Middle American Anthropology: Directory,*

Bibliography, and Guide to the UCLA Library Collection. 1975.

Griffin, Charles C., ed. *Latin America: A Guide to the Historical Literature.* 1971.

Handbook of Latin American Studies.

American Historical Association. *Guide to Historical Literature.* 1961.

Users of this guide may want to use White as a reference tool for an overview of general anthropological literature sources and McGlynn for an introduction to Middle American anthropological literature. Griffin's work provides an overview of materials relating specifically to Latin America, and the *Handbook of Latin American Studies* complements and updates Griffin. For a historian's perspective, the American Historical Association Guide is useful.

1. White, Carl M., and associates. *Sources of Information in the Social Sciences: A Guide to the Literature.* 2nd ed. Chicago: American Library Association, 1973.

This is a major comprehensive guide to social science literature. Its strong point is that each major section was written by a subject specialist. Each section is divided into subsections that cover the basic works and the guides to the literature in the field. Users of this guide should refer to the chapter on anthropology as well as to the index.

2. McGlynn, Eileen A. *Middle American Anthropology: Directory, Bibliography, and Guide to the UCLA Library Collections.* Los Angeles: Latin American Center and University Library, University of California, 1975.

This work bridges an important gap between the anthropology guides and the Latin American guides. It is a very important introductory source to library resources for Middle American anthropology. The sources included are not restricted to holdings in the UCLA collection.

The guide is divided into two sections: Section 1, "Middle American Anthropological Research: A Directory of Major Contributors," covers people and institutions prominent in the development of Middle American studies. Section 2, "Sources on Middle American Anthropology," covers reference and bibliographic sources; journals, series, and proceedings; selected books and monographs; and rare and non-book materials.

An author-title index is included for the work as a whole and a geographic and chronological index is provided for the selected books and monographs section.

This is a remarkable publication and deserves to be constantly referred to regardless of whether or not one has access to the UCLA library collections.

3. Griffin, Charles C., ed. *Latin America: A Guide to the Historical Literature.* Austin: University of Texas Press, 1971.

Pertinent information can be located in Griffin's work by consulting Part III.A ("Background: Archaeology"), which is an annotated bibliography compiled by Robert Wauchope. Though Wauchope states that his list of books and periodical articles is intended for the nonspecialist or beginning reader in archaeology, graduate students should find Wauchope's evaluative annotations of international publications quite useful. Information specific to Mesoamerican archaeology can be found in the "Archaeology: General" and "Archaeology: Middle America" sections. Entries are arranged alphabetically by author, and an author index is provided. The cutoff date for inclusion is 1966. As mentioned previously, Griffin also provides a section on ethnohistory.

4. *Handbook of Latin American Studies.* Gainesville: University of Florida Press, No. 1-, 1935-. Annual.

This annual publication is a select and annotated bibliography, prepared by scholars, of recently published books, periodical articles, pamphlets, etc. on various topics relating to Latin America. Coverage varies or alternates by year; one year the social sciences will be covered; the next year, the humanities. As already mentioned, an ethnohistory section for Mesoamerica is included. For information on Mesoamerican archaeology, turn to the "Archaeology: Mesoamerica" section of the social sciences volume. Entries are classed according to subtopics ("General," "Excavations and Artifacts," and "Native Sources"). Within each subtopic, the entries are arranged alphabetically by author. Complete bibliographic information is included. Length of the annotations varies; some are descriptive, others are critical or evaluative. A subject index is included at the end of each volume.

In 1968, Francisco José and María Elena Cardona compiled a cumulative author index for the 1936-1966 issues of the *Handbook.*

5. American Historical Association. *Guide to Historical Literature.* New York: Macmillan, 1961.

This work provides an overview of pre-1961 publications on various topics in history. Each chapter was written by subject experts and includes a selective, annotated bibliography of the topic. Users of this guide may wish to refer to sections E 84-124 ("Regions, Peoples, and Cultures: General and Prehistoric: The New World") as well as sections Y ("The Americas") and Z ("Latin America"). This work includes, in one volume, most of the core literature published prior to 1961.

BIBLIOGRAPHIES

Researchers interested in Mesoamerican archaeology will find bibliographies, both retrospective and current, to be invaluable aids in locating material that is scattered through the anthropological literature and the literature of other fields. Bibliographies will be found to exist in a variety of formats: monographs, parts of books, parts of articles, and catalogs of special collections. No attempt has been made to determine, per volume cited, the number of bibliographic listings germane to Mesoamerican archaeology. However, all of the listings contain substantial quantities of such information.

Retrospective Bibliographies

The following retrospective bibliographies are especially valuable:

Gropp, Arthur E., comp. *A Bibliography of Latin American Bibliographies.* 1968.

Bernal, Ignacio. *Bibliografía de arqueología y etnografía: Mesoamérica y norte de México, 1514-1960.* 1962.

Comas, Juan. *Bibliografía selectiva de las culturas indígenas de América.* 1953.

Harvard University Library. Widener Library Shelflist, No. 5. *Latin America and Latin American Periodicals.* 1966.

Gropp is useful for locating lists of bibliographies relating to Mesoamerican archaeology in its many facets. Bernal's work, truly a classic, is the most comprehensive coverage (retrospectively as well as internationally) of the topic. Comas has selected mostly English-language publications to include in his bibliography. The Harvard work provides a classified means of locating pertinent materials. For further sources of bibliographies, consult the reference and bibliography section of McGlynn (2).

6. Gropp, Arthur E., comp. *A Bibliography of Latin American Bibliographies.* Metuchen, New Jersey: Scarecrow Press, 1968.

Gropp's bibliography of bibliographies is concerned with 7,210 bibliographies in monographic form, published throughout the world. Organization is by subject arrangement, with area subdivisions where applicable. For bibliographies centering on Mesoamerican archaeology, turn to the "Archaeology" section. Other sections of interest are "Maps" and "Anthropology." Within each of these sections, each main subject group is arranged by country; entries are listed alphabetically by author. Although annotations are scarce, complete bibliographic information is provided. This work is accompanied by a detailed index of authors, titles, and subjects.

To supplement and update this bibliography, Gropp compiled *A Bibliography of Latin American Bibliographies: Supplement, 1971* (Metuchen, New Jersey: Scarecrow Press, 1971). This *Supplement* follows the same arrangement as the 1968 work.

As a companion volume, to cover bibliographies published in periodicals (especially Latin American periodicals), Gropp compiled *A Bibliography of Latin American Bibliographies Published in Periodicals* (Metuchen, New Jersey: Scarecrow Press, 1976). Coverage focuses, for the most part, on bibliographies published in periodicals between 1929 and 1965.

7. Bernal, Ignacio. *Bibliografía de arqueología y etnografía: Mesoamérica y norte de México, 1514-1960.* Mexico City: Instituto Nacional de Antropología e Historia, 1962.

Perhaps the bibliography of greatest value to users of this guide is Bernal's classic compilation. This work boasts nearly 14,000 entries and is international in its coverage of monographic and serial publications covering five centuries of archaeological and ethnological materials on Mesoamerica. The arrangement of this material is by geographic culture areas, with subdivisions for general information, sites, objects, ethnography, religion, etc. Users should be aware that the Table of Contents is located at the back of the volume, it is essential for directing the user to the different sections of the book. An author index is provided.

Within each section, arrangement is alphabetical by author. Complete bibliographic information is given; however, there are no annotations. Two fold-out maps are provided to indicate the areas included in the bibliography. When pertinent, citations are made to book reviews and to translations of certain works.

8. Comas, Juan. *Bibliografía selectiva de las culturas indígenas de América.* Mexico City: Instituto Panamericano de Geografía e Historia, 1953.

This work, unlike Bernal's, lists mostly English-title books, monographic series, and periodical articles. Since Comas has adopted a classified arrangement for this work, refer to his "Origen del hombre americano: Área cultural: Mesoamérica" section. Within this section, the 258 listings are arranged alphabetically by author. There is a general index of indigenous peoples and one of authors. A few culture area maps are also included.

9. Harvard University Library. Widener Library Shelflist, No. 5. *Latin America and Latin American Periodicals.* 2 vols. Cambridge, Massachusetts: Harvard University Library, 1966.

Researchers will be pleasantly surprised by the arrangement of this catalog. Using the Widener Library shelflist, the Harvard University staff compiled this classified catalog. In the first volume, *Classification Schedule and Classified Listing by Call Number,* works on Mexican and Middle American archaeology are all *brought together* under class SA 3800-3807. Scan through the classification outline to locate other possibilities.

The second volume of this set provides author, title, and chronological (ca. 1521-1966) listings.

Current Bibliographies

Current bibliographies provide a quick survey of what has recently been published in the field. To update the retrospective bibliographies that have just been discussed, users of this guide will wish to consult:

Bibliographic Index
International Bibliography of Social and Cultural Anthropology
Index to Literature on the American Indian
Boletín Bibliográfico de Antropología Americana (B.B.A.A.)

The *Bibliographic Index* serves to update Gropp. The *International Bibliography of Social and Cultural Anthropology* focuses more specifically on publications from around the world that deal with the archaeology of America, while the *Index to Literature on the American Indian* is more concerned with locating English-language publications. Also, as previously discussed, the *Handbook of Latin American Studies* (4) provides, on an annual basis, annotations of newly published bibliographies relevant to Latin America. Each issue of the *Boletín Bibliográfico de Antropología Americana (B.B.A.A.)* contains a bibliography of recently published works.

10. *Bibliographic Index: A Cumulative Bibliography of Bibliographies.* New York: H. W. Wilson Company, v. 1-, 1937-.

This alphabetically arranged list of bibliographies covers Germanic- and Romance-language bibliographies that have been published separately or as parts of books, pamphlets, and periodicals. Its value lies in its currentness. It is published three times a year–April, August, and, in a bound cumulation, in December. To find information on Mesoamerican archaeology, use the standard Library of Congress subject headings and make use of the *See also* references.

11. *International Bibliography of Social and Cultural Anthropology.* London: Tavistock Publications; Chicago: Aldine Publishing, v. 1-, 1955-. Annual.

This is an attempt to bring together, on an annual basis, international publications (journal articles, books, reports, government publications), etc. dealing with various facets of anthropology. Despite the work's title, information on Mesoamerican archaeology can be pinpointed in the subject index (under "Archaeology: America") at the end of each volume. The *See also* references at the beginning of each section direct the user to further entries of interest. An author index is also provided for each issue.

Within each section, entries are arranged alphabetically by author. Complete bibliographic information is provided, but there are no annotations.

Note: This work is a component of the *International Bibliography of the Social Sciences* series; there is always a publication time-lag of a few years.

12. *Index to Literature on the American Indian.* San Francisco: Indian Historian Press, v. 1-, 1971-.

This annual publication is intended to cover a fair sampling of popular and scholarly American publications (books and periodical articles) dealing with native Americans. Arrangement is alphabetical by subject and alphabetical by author within each major subject grouping. Special sections to note are: "Bibliographies," "Audio-Visuals," "Archaeology," "Book Reviews," "Ethnohistory," and "Indian Tribes–Mexico and Central America." The section on Indian tribes subdivides the groups linguistically.

Although no annotations are provided, complete bibliographic details are given.

13. *Boletín Bibliográfico de Antropología Americana (B.B.A.A.).* Mexico City: Comisión de Historia del Instituto Panamericano de Geografía e Historia, v. 1-, 1937-.

Although this publication suffers from a publication time-lag, it is very useful for the wealth and diversity of information contained. Samples taken from the Table of Contents include current news on anthropological and archaeological activities in institutions throughout the world; investigations and studies by specialists in the field; biographies and bibliographies by individuals on certain topics; book reviews; obituary information; and a bibliography of recently published works.

PERIODICALS

Directories

Periodicals may provide the most up-to-date articles on recent research. The task of a periodical directory is to provide bibliographic, publishing, and ordering details. They are usually arranged by subject or by country. The following directories should prove to be of value:

Ulrich's International Periodicals Directory.

Irregular Serials and Annuals.

Tax, Sol, and Grolling, Francis X., eds. *Serial Publications in Anthropology.* 1973.

Zimmerman, Irene. *A Guide to Current Latin American Periodicals: Humanities and Social Sciences.* 1961.

Levi, Nadia. *Guía de publicaciones periódicas de universidades latinoamericanas.* 1967.

These selections were chosen to complement one another. *Ulrich's* is strong in its international coverage of publications that are issued more than once a year; *Irregular Serials and Annuals* covers those issued annually or less frequently. *Serial Publications in Anthropology* is an attempt to gain control over anthropological serial publications. Zimmerman's *Guide* provides various approaches to information on periodicals issued by Latin American countries. Levi's work provides a country-by-country breakdown of periodicals published in Latin America. The Harvard University Widener Shelflist (9), section SAP, lists Latin American periodicals. SAP 801-950 alphabetically lists periodicals published in Mexico; SAP 1001-1150 lists those published in Central America. McGlynn (2) also lists periodicals and serials that deal with Mesoamerican anthropology.

14. *Ulrich's International Periodicals Directory: A Classified Guide to Current Periodicals, Foreign and Domestic.* New York: R. R. Bowker, ed. 1-, 1932-.

This biennial publication provides a helpful classified listing of 57,000 titles of periodicals issued more than once a year, published throughout the world. For periodical titles relating to archaeology, use the "Key to Subjects" in front of the book to locate the "Archaeology" and "Anthropology" sections. Arrangement of entries is then alphabetical by title. Information for each entry includes the name of the publisher, publisher's current address, date of origin, frequency, price, and, most important, where it is indexed or abstracted. Also included are a list of periodicals that have ceased publication and indexes to publications of international organizations. A title index is also provided.

15. *Irregular Serials and Annuals: An International Directory.* New York: R. R. Bowker, ed. 1967-.

This biennial companion to Ulrich's provides bibliographic and purchasing information for almost 30,000 serials published throughout the world. It covers serials, conference proceedings, transactions, yearbooks, reports, handbooks, annual reviews, and monographic series. This work includes foreign and domestic publications that are issued irregularly, annually, or less frequently than once a year. To locate listings of this nature, use the same approach as outlined for *Ulrich's*. This work also provides information on cessations and indexes to publications of international organizations.

Samples of listings:

Atlas arqueológico de la República Mexicana

Peabody Museum of Archaeology and Ethnology. Papers.
Cerámica de cultura maya

16. Tax, Sol, and Grolling, Francis X., eds. *Serial Publications in Anthropology.* Chicago: University of Chicago Press, 1973.

This is an alphabetical listing by main entry of serial publications that nine institutions in Chicago identified as being of primary interest to anthropologists. Nothing else like it exists; it is truly remarkable. It is comprehensive (there are more than 3,000 entries) and international in scope.

For each listing, the following information is provided: publisher's name, address, frequency of publication, language of publication, and, if applicable, where the publication is indexed or abstracted.

One major drawback is that there is no subject or geographic access to this book.

The editors hope to regularly update this publication.

17. Zimmerman, Irene. *A Guide to Current Latin American Periodicals: Humanities and Social Sciences.* Gainesville, Florida: Kallman Publishing Company, 1961.

This book provides a collective listing of publications issued by twenty-seven Latin American countries. One of its strengths is that various approach avenues are available: national, subject, title, and chronological. In addition, the author provides an evaluative annotation, written in English, for each periodical listed. Check the anthropology subject section for a list of periodicals relating to this field, and then read the annotations in the national section.

Other important features of this work include Zimmerman's "Casualty List" for cessations and her suggestions as to how to evaluate Latin American periodicals.

18. Levi, Nadia. *Guía de publicaciones periódicas de universidades latinoamericanos.* Mexico City: Universidad Nacional Autónoma de México, 1967.

This work is a listing of 1,068 periodical titles published in Latin American countries. Arrangement is by country. Information per entry includes title, initial publication date, full bibliographic data, and frequency. There are no annotations. The Table of Contents at the *end* of the volume does provide subject access, but there are no subject headings for either anthropology or archaeology. A section on university publications may be of some help.

Levi should be used to supplement Zimmerman—Levi's work contains many more listings, but Zimmerman provides annotations.

Journals

Periodicals that are of outstanding value to students working in Mesoamerican archaeology include:

19. *American Antiquity.* vol. 1-, 1935-. Washington, D.C.: Society for American Archaeology. Quarterly.
20. *American Anthropologist.* v. 1-, 1888-. Washington, D.C.: American Anthropological Association. Quarterly.
21. *Journal of Field Archaeology.* v. 1-, 1974-. Boston: Boston University Association for Field Archaeology. Quarterly.
22. *Journal de la Société des Américanistes de Paris.* v. 1-, 1895-. Paris: Société des Américanistes. Semiannually.
23. *Katunob.* v. 1-, 1960-. Greeley, Colorado: University of Northern Colorado. Quarterly.
24. *World Archaeology.* v. 1-, 1969-. London: Routledge and Kegan Paul, Ltd. 3/yr.

Indexes

Periodical indexes provide a means of locating recent articles published in periodical literature. These indexes should be consulted on a regular basis in order to maintain contact with recent research. The following indexes are pertinent to the topic of this guide:

Social Sciences Index and *Humanities Index.*

Pan American Union. Columbus Memorial Library. *Index to Latin American Periodical Literature, 1929-1960.*

Indice general de publicaciones periódicas latinoamericanas: Humanidades y ciencias sociales. Index to Latin American Periodicals: Humanities and Social Sciences. Issued quarterly between 1961 and 1970; no volumes have since been issued.

Hispanic American Periodicals Index. 1974; 1975-.
Anthropological Index to Current Periodicals Received in the Library of the Royal Anthropological Institute. 1963-.
Comas, Juan. *Indices generales de Anales de Antropología, Vols. I-XII, Años 1964-1974.* 1975.

The *Social Sciences Index* and the *Humanities Index* will aid students of Mesoamerican archaeology in locating current English-language periodical articles. The Columbus Memorial Library catalog provides information on articles published in Latin American periodicals between 1929 and 1968 and uses subject headings written in English. The *Indice general* updates the Columbus library catalog to 1970 and also covers INAH publications. The *Hispanic American Periodicals Index,* in turn, updates the *Indice general.* The Royal Institute's *Anthropological Index* is issued four times each year and is international in scope. Comas's work is a specialized index to the *Anales* of the Universidad Nacional Autónoma de México (UNAM). Note also that *Ulrich's* (14), *Irregular Serials* (15), and *Serial Publications in Anthropology* (16) provide information under each title as to who indexes the publication.

Serious researchers may also be able to use the *Social Sciences Citations Index*'s *Permuterm Subject Index* (84) to locate recent journal articles.

25. *Social Sciences Index* and *Humanities Index.* New York: H. W. Wilson, v. 1-, 1907-. Quarterly.

Various title changes have occurred through the years with this publication. From 1907 to 1955 it was known as the *International Index,* and from 1955 to 1974 it was called the *Social Sciences and Humanities Index.* In April, 1974, the publishers split this title into two separate indexes: the *Social Sciences Index* and the *Humanities Index.*

The value of these indexes, which use an author/subject dictionary arrangement, is that researchers are provided with a quarterly index that covers articles in hundreds of social science and humanities periodicals. Cumulations are made for every other volume and at the end of the year.

Also, beginning with the April 1974 volume, there is an author listing of citations to book reviews following the main body of the index.

Use the standard Library of Congress subject headings as access points.

Researchers will wish to consult *both* the *Social Sciences Index* and the *Humanities Index.* There is very little overlap between them.

26. Pan American Union. Columbus Memorial Library. *Index to Latin American Periodical Literature, 1929-1960.* Boston: G. K. Hall, 1962. 1st supplement, 1961-1965, was published in 1968.

These multiple volumes provide subject access, via photoduplicated catalog cards of the Columbus Memorial Library of the Pan American Union, to articles published in Latin American periodicals between 1919 and 1965. The criterion for inclusion was that the periodical article contain information pertinent to subjects relating to Latin America. For the most part, coverage is of periodicals of Latin American origin. Periodicals published outside of Latin America are included when they contain information about Latin America or were written by Latin American authors.

Arrangement is by subject and, for works published after 1951, by author. Consult the standard list of LC subject headings and the cross references.

27. *Indice general de publicaciones periódicas latinoamericanas: Humanidades y ciencias sociales. Index to Latin American Periodicals: Humanities and Social Sciences,* prepared by the Columbus Memorial Library, Pan American Union. Metuchen, New Jersey: Scarecrow Press, vols. 1-10, April 1961-June 1970.

These volumes, covering more than two hundred Latin American periodicals, serve to update the *Index to Latin American Periodical Literature* (26) as far as 1970. Originally published by the G. K. Hall Company, the publishing rights have been transferred to Scarecrow Press. Read the introduction (in any of the volumes) to understand the change in arrangement that occurred with the transfer.

For example, volumes 1 and 2 have an author, subject, title, dictionary arrangement. With volume 3 a new pattern was implemented—articles are grouped under subject headings, and cross references and an annual author index are provided.

Unfortunately, there is no subject or title cumulation for the quarters; users must search each of the four sections of a volume. Subject headings are written in Spanish. English equivalents are given at the end of each volume.

This work provides good coverage of INAH publications and of many other anthropological/archaeological publications.

Students of Mesoamerican archaeology will wish to use the subject headings:

Country–ANTIGÜEDADES
INDIOS–Various Subheadings
INVESTIGACIÓN ARQUEOLÓGICA
ARQUEOLOGÍA
Anything else that comes to mind

28. Cox, Barbara, ed. *Hispanic American Periodicals Index: Cumulative Index, 1974.* Tempe, Arizona: Arizona State University, 1974.

This index, commonly referred to as *HAPI*, is a selective author/subject index to almost one hundred English, Spanish, and Portuguese language periodicals covering Latin America. The articles selected for inclusion are those currently received at Arizona State University. Many of these publications are not indexed elsewhere.

The chief value of this index is that it updates the Pan American Union's *Index* (26) and the *Indice general* (27). It also includes a book review section.

Authors' names and subject headings are arranged in one alphabet. Use the standard LC subject headings.

To update this 1974 issue of *HAPI*, consult Cox's *Hispanic American Periodicals Index, 1975* (Los Angeles: UCLA Latin American Center Publications, 1977).

This book serves to bring Cox's 1974 index up to date by covering articles appearing in 1975 in more than two hundred major journals published in Central and South America, Mexico, the United States, Europe, and the Caribbean.

Arrangement is by subject (using LC subject headings) and by author. Book reviews are listed in the subject section by author of the book reviewed. Reviews of films can also be found in the subject section under "Film Reviews."

The UCLA Latin American Center plans to issue such an index each year, which will make this a very important bibliographic tool for Latin American researchers. Citations for this index have been stored in machine-readable form, and future plans include the offering of individualized retrospective data searches.

29. *Anthropological Index to Current Periodicals Received in the Library of the Royal Anthropological Institute.* London: Royal Anthropological Institute of Great Britain and Ireland, v. 1-, January/March 1963-. Quarterly.

This index is important because it provides a way to update the *International Bibliography of Social and Cultural Anthropology* (11), which is always rather late in being published.

This publication covers more than five hundred periodicals received by the Museum of Mankind Library and the Royal Anthropological Institute Library. It is international in scope. A list of the periodicals indexed by this publication can be found in volume 6, part 4, pp. 146-155. Additions and amendments to the current periodicals indexed are summarized at the beginning of each issue.

Arrangement of this publication is by geographic location. The "General" section lists obituaries and biographies. In the early issues (i.e., 1963-71), to locate information on Mesoamerican archaeology look up "America: Archaeology" in the Table of Contents of each issue. For 1972 and subsequent issues, look in the Table of Contents for "America: Central America" and then locate the Archaeology section.

No cumulative index exists for these volumes. However, beginning with the 1972 issue (volume 10), each volume carries its own author index.

30. Comas, Juan. *Indices generales de Anales de Antropología, Vols. I-XII, Años 1964-1974.* Mexico City: Instituto de Investigaciones Antropológicas de la Universidad Nacional Autónoma de México, 1975.

Comas has compiled an index to authors of articles, bibliographies, etc. that were published in the *Anales* of UNAM. Arrangement is alphabetical by surname. He also provides a subject index to articles written about American archaeology, prehistory, and ethnohistory.

ABSTRACTS

Abstracts are important time-savers to the researcher as they provide descriptive or indicative information on an article. Abstracts for anthropological articles have been available since 1940, with the first issue of *Bulletin Signalétique.* However, the only abstracting service to focus exclusively on Mesoamerica and the rest of the New World was *Abstracts of New World Archaeology,* which, unfortunately, lasted only two years (1959 to 1960). More recently, *Abstracts in Anthropology* has been published to cover the entire field of anthropology and its many subdisciplines.

The following are major sources for abstracts of literature relevant to Mesoamerican archaeology:

Abstracts in Anthropology
Abstracts of New World Archaeology
Bulletin Signalétique, Sec. 525, Préhistoire, and Sec. 526, *Art et Archéologie.*

Consult both *Abstracts in Anthropology* and *Bulletin Signalétique* for the most recent coverage. As mentioned above, *Abstracts of New World Archaeology* covers only those publications that appeared in 1959 and 1960. Remember that that *Ulrich's* (14), *Irregular Serials* (15), and *Serial Publications in Anthropology* (16), although they do not provide abstracts per se, provide information on where abstracts may be found for certain periodical titles.

31. *Abstracts in Anthropology.* Farmingdale, New York: Baywood Publishing Company, v. 1-, 1970-.

These quarterly publications are intended to provide summary information of current anthropological literature. They cover journal and periodical articles as well as papers presented at meetings. Coverage is slanted heavily toward English language publications.

Prior to the Fall 1973 issue, one must locate the archaeology section of each volume and scan through its contents to find appropriate materials. However, with the Fall 1973 and subsequent issues, the Table of Contents directs the user to a section on "Archaeology: Mesoamerica." Additional information can be gleaned by using the author or subject index located at the end of each volume (check under specific names of Indian groups as well as under "Archaeology–Aspects of," etc.).

The abstracts, written in English, are rather short and usually provide descriptive rather than analytical information. Each abstract does, however, cite full bibliographical information.

At one time an annual subject and author index was planned for this work. As yet, it has not been forthcoming.

32. Woodbury, Richard B., ed. *Abstracts of New World Archaeology.* Washington, D.C.: Society for American Archaeology, v. 1-2, 1959-1960.

Although only two issues of this work ever materialized, it is still valuable for its abstracts covering publications issued throughout the world for the years 1959 and 1960. The focus is New World archaeology; use the Table of Contents to pinpoint more specific geographic areas in Mesoamerica. Entries are arranged alphabetically within geographic regions. Complete bibliographic information is provided. The abstracts vary in length and are usually only descriptive. An author index accompanies each volume.

Scholars should note that this work also includes abstracts of unpublished theses and dissertations.

33. *Bulletin Signalétique.* Sec. 526. *Art et Archéologie: Proche Orient-Asie-Amérique.* Paris: Centre de Documentation Sciences Humaines, v. 1-, 1940-.

This quarterly publication has a number of important features. It can be used as an index to current periodical literature and to abstracts and reviews. The entire publication is written in French, but the scope is international. Since the arrangement of the bulletin is classified, use the "Plan de Classement" to locate the section on "Civilisations Américaines." Indexes are provided for concepts, subjects, and authors. There are also sections entitled "Liste des Revues Dépouillées" and "Liste Cumulative des Revues."

Information per entry includes author, title, and other bibliographic information; an abstract written in French; and, if it is a book, a citation reference to where it has been provided.

For pre-1970 publications of this work, refer to White (1) for an explanation of the different formats.

To supplement this bulletin, consult also:

Bulletin Signalétique. Sec. 525. *Préhistoire.*

This is another publication issued quarterly by the Paris

documentation center. It provides the same arrangement, style, and features.

For information on Mesoamerican archaeology, again consult the "Plan de Classement" and locate the "Amérique et Régions Arctiques: Mexique et Amérique Centrale" section.

This *Bulletin* provides indexes of cultures, geographic regions, sites in the regions, materials (des matières) as well as a "Table des Auteurs," a "Liste Cumulative des Revues," and a "Liste des Revues Dépouillées."

REVIEWS

Reviews of anthropological literature can be located in a variety of sources. For publications issued between 1959 and 1960, check the *Biennial Review of Anthropology.* For works issued after 1972, consult the *Annual Review of Anthropology.* A basic guide to post-1965 book reviews covering Latin America is Matos's *Guía a las reseñas de libros de y sobre Hispanoamérica.* Book reviews are also important features of the *Bulletin Signalétique* (33), *Boletín Bibliográfico de Antropología Americana* (13), and the journals *American Antiquity* (19) and *American Anthropologist* (20). As may be recalled, Bernal's *Bibliografía* (7), the *Index to Literature on the American Indian* (12), the *Social Sciences Index* and the *Humanities Index* (25), and Cox's *Hispanic American Periodicals Index* (28) all carry sections referring researchers to sources of book reviews for various works. In addition, the *Social Sciences Citation Index* (84) may also be used to locate book reviews (see the "Search Techniques" section of this guide.)

34. Siegel, Bernard J., ed. *Biennial Review of Anthropology.* Stanford: Stanford University Press, 1959-1971.

This biennial publication was designed to provide reviews, written by specialists, of relevant anthropological literature (papers and monographs) so that anthropologists could keep up with their field. Some of the volumes do contain review articles dealing with Mesoamerican archaeology. To locate such reviews, check the Table of Contents and the subject indexes in each volume. These reviews are important in tracing the research history of the field as well as in providing international retrospective bibliographies. This work ceased publication in 1971 and is continued by the *Annual Review of Anthropology* (35).

35. Siegel, Bernard J., ed. *Annual Review of Anthropology.* Palo Alto,

California: Annual Reviews, Inc., v. 1-, 1972-.

Designed to continue the *Biennial Review of Anthropology* (34), the papers presented in this annual publication serve to provide anthropologists with survey review articles of recently published materials. The reviews, written by specialists, cover the various subdisciplines of anthropology. Each volume devotes at least one lengthy review article to a topic in archaeology and usually covers something on Mesoamerican archaeology. Each paper is accompanied by a substantial bibliography of the international literature cited. (The subject index in each volume will direct users to information on the archaeology of Mesoamerica. An author index is also included.)

Each volume also contains cumulative indexes of contributing authors and of chapter titles. Volume 5 contains a cumulative index of contributing authors and of subjects/chapter titles for volumes 1-5. Volume 6 has a cumulative subjects/chapter titles index for volumes 2-6.

36. Matos, Antonio, ed. *Guía a las reseñas de libros de y sobre Hispanoamérica.* Detroit: Blaine Ethridge Books, 1965-.

When this guide began publication in 1965, it provided only an author/title list of books relating to Latin America and published throughout the world. References were given as to where reviews of the books could be found. This first edition covered the years 1960-1964. No further editions were forthcoming until 1976, when the volumes covering the years 1972 and 1973 were issued. These volumes fill an important gap by bringing the 1965 issue up to date and by providing annotations of the reviews. The annotations are usually written in English.

Arrangement of all editions is alphabetical by author of the book being reviewed. Title indexes are provided.

NEWSFORMS

Newspapers and newsletters are important sources of current information and organizational news. Unfortunately, few indexes of such publications exist. Listed below are one newspaper index and one newsletter, both of which include information pertinent to the topic of this guide. These should be consulted and read on a regular basis. In addition, one directory of newsletters is given as an example.

New York Times Index
Anthropology Newsletter
Standard Directory of Newsletters

37. *New York Times Index.* New York: New York Times Company, v. 1-, 1851-.

This index to the *New York Times* is arranged alphabetically by subject. Each entry provides a short summary of the article and a reference to the date, page, and column in the *NYT*. The index is now published twice each month, with an annual cumulation.

This work is important for its current information on the latest field discoveries by Mesoamerican archaeologists. Locate this information by using the subject headings

ARCHAEOLOGY AND ANTHROPOLOGY–Name of Indian group
ARCHAEOLOGY AND ANTHROPOLOGY–Name of country

38. *Anthropology Newsletter.* Washington, D.C.: American Anthropological Association, v. 1-, 1947-.

This official newsletter of the AAA is issued ten times each year. Each issue contains information on the activities of the AAA, as well as the activities of other organizations. Important sections are those covering grants and support, conference dates, placement, and general announcements.

39. *Standard Directory of Newsletters.* 1st ed. New York: Oxbridge Publishing, 1972.

Although few of the listings in this directory are of newsletters directly covering Mesoamerican archaeology, it is valuable as the only source of current bibliographical information on newsletters. These newsforms represent one of the best sources of current information on an organization, but, unfortunately, they are ephemeral. Nonetheless, this *Standard Directory* does provide a sampling of the types of newsletters that cover anthropology and archaeology.

Arrangement of this directory is classified–use the Table of Contents to locate pertinent sections. A cross-index to subjects is also available. Arrangement within each section is alphabetical by title, and complete bibliographic information is included. Note the *See also* references.

In addition, many Latin American institutes publish newsletters to keep Mesoamericanists up to date. Examples of such publications are the newsletters of the Institute of Latin American Studies of The University of Texas at Austin and the Latin American Studies Association in Gainesville, Florida. Information of these institutes may be located by referring to Palmer's *Research Centers Directory* (48).

THESES AND DISSERTATIONS

Information in theses and dissertations is of vital concern to archaeologists because this is often the only time that the results of fieldwork are published. Moreover, they provide access to the very latest research. Often, copies of dissertations are available for purchase on microfilm.

Indexes to dissertations and theses go as far back as 1861. Work has been done on compiling comprehensive national lists as well as specialized subject lists. Though there is no list that pertains solely to Mesoamerican archaeology, the following works provide means of access to pertinent documents.

Comprehensive Dissertation Index

Dissertation Abstracts International

Dockstader, Frederick J., and Dockstader, Alice W. *The American Indian in Graduate Studies: A Bibliography of Theses and Dissertations,* 2nd ed.

Yearbook of Anthropology, 1955

Users of this guide will wish to refer to the *Comprehensive Dissertation Index (CDI)* for dissertations written prior to 1972. *Dissertation Abstracts International (DAI)* supplements *CDI* by providing abstracts and by bringing the list up to the present. Dockstader is used as a subject approach to theses and dissertations written in schools in the United States, Canada, and Mexico. The *Yearbook of Anthropology,* which is updated by certain issues of *Current Anthropology,* supplies information on dissertations written at institutions throughout the world. Remember that *Abstracts of New World Archaeology* (32) includes abstracts of unpublished Master's and Ph.D. documents for the years 1959 and 1960.

In addition, the Center for Research Libraries in Chicago[10] currently houses a collection of over 600,000 titles of foreign doctoral dissertations that are available for loan to member institutions. If a certain title is not in their collection, the Center will order a copy and send it to the requester.

For an annual list of dissertation titles and the names of students who were granted Ph.D.s, check the current issue of the American Anthropological Association's *Guide to Departments of Anthropology* (76).

40. *Comprehensive Dissertation Index, 1861-1972.* Ann Arbor: Xerox University Microfilms, 1973.

This work lists 417,000 dissertations, written between 1861 and 1972, for which doctoral degrees were granted by educational institutions in the United States. Some dissertations accepted by foreign universities have also been included. Annual supplements bring the work up to 1974.

Users of this guide will wish to refer to volume 17, which covers the social sciences. Since arrangement is by key words, look for the headings "Archaeological," "Archaeology," "Prehistory," and for names of regions, countries, and Indian groups.

Full citations appear for each entry, including a reference to the volume and page number in *Dissertation Abstracts International* (41).

If an author is already known, consult the author indexes, volumes 33 through 37.

This publication is currently one of the System Development Corporation's data bases. This means that it is machine searchable through SDC's ORBIT data base management system. Your local librarian will be able to tell you more about on-line data base searching.

41. *Dissertation Abstracts International.* Ann Arbor: University Microfilms, v. 1-, 1938-.

These volumes, issued monthly, provide abstracts of doctoral dissertations that were submitted to University Microfilms by universities in the United States and abroad. For dissertations written prior to 1924, it may be easier to locate the volume and page number of a dissertation title in *DAI* by using the *Comprehensive Dissertation Index* (40).

For access to abstract information on very recent dissertations, turn to the latest volumes of *Dissertation Abstracts: Series A: Humanities and Social Sciences* and locate the anthropology and archaeology sections. Other approaches are to use the keyword title index or the author index located at the back of each volume.

All abstracts are microfilmed by University Microfilms and are available for purchase. Purchasing information is provided in each issue of *DAI.*

42. Dockstader, Frederick J., and Dockstader, Alice W. *The American Indian in Graduate Studies: A Bibliography of Theses and Dissertations,* 2nd ed. New York: Museum of the American Indian, Heye Foundation, 1973; 1974.

This bibliography lists theses and dissertations, submitted to colleges and universities in the United States, Canada, and Mexico, that pertain to the American Indian. The 1973 edition covers the years 1890 to 1955; the 1974 supplement brings this coverage up to 1970. Together, these two volumes list 7,471 titles.

In each volume, works are listed alphabetically by author, and each author is given an accession number. The 1974 volume provides a subject index that covers both the 1973 and the 1974 volumes. Along with major subheadings such as "Archaeology: Middle America," archaeological sites are also indexed.

43. *Yearbook of Anthropology, 1955.* New York: Wenner-Gren Foundation for Anthropological Research, 1955.

This publication, a one-shot affair, is valuable for its listing of Ph.D. dissertation titles in anthropology for which degrees were awarded between the years 1870 and 1954 at institutions throughout the world. Arrangement is alphabetical by institution, then chronological by year of award. No subject approach exists.

This list is supplemented by the following issues of *Current Anthropology: A World Journal of the Sciences of Man* (New York: Wenner-Gren Foundation):

1966, vol. 7, pp. 606-627
1968, vol. 9, pp. 590-606
1970, vol. 11, p. 234

ASSOCIATIONS AND SOCIETIES

Anthropological associations exist throughout the world. Contact with, or membership in, one of these associations or societies may confer many privileges.

For example, members are usually provided with issues of journals, newsletters, and other printed materials, and they are notified of conventions and conferences to be held. Also, one's name is often put on mailing lists, an important way to find out about trade publications.

Some anthropological associations and publications that are especially concerned with Mesoamerican archaeology are:

American Anthropological Association
American Anthropologist
Society for American Archaeology
American Antiquity
Société des Américanistes
Journal de la Société des Américanistes
Bibliographie Américaniste
Sociedad Mexicana de Antropología
Revista Mexicana de Estudios Antropológicos
American Philosophical Society
Transactions of the American Philosophical Society

Information about these and other associations can be found in the following sources:

International Directory of Anthropological Institutions. 1953.
"Fourth International Directory of Anthropological Institutions," in *Current Anthropology,* 1967.
Encyclopedia of Associations
Bosch García, Carlos. *Guía de instituciones que cultivan la historia de América.* 1949.

McGlynn (2) also supplies information on Middle American anthropological associations, both domestic and foreign. The *International Bibliography of Social and Cultural Anthropology* (11) provides information on recent publications stemming from anthropological meetings.

44. Thomas, William L., and Pikelis, Anna M. *International Directory of Anthropological Institutions.* New York: Wenner-Gren Foundation for Anthropological Research, 1953.

Although the data pertaining to officers in this book is quite out of date, the book is valuable for its list of anthropological institutions. For each institution (educational, research, museum, professional association) listed, directory-type information is provided. Although there is an index to institutions, cities, towns, there is no subject index.

45. "Fourth International Directory of Anthropological Institutions," in *Current Anthropology* 8 (December 1967, part 2):647-751.

This issue of *Current Anthropology* is the most recent update of Thomas's directory (44). Arrangement and type of information is the same. International bodies are covered, along with professional societies, museums, and research institutions. Information for each includes name, address, areas of interest, professional staff, awards, research aid available, publications, and membership requirements.

46. *Encyclopedia of Associations.* Detroit: Gale Research Company, ed. 1-, 1956-.

The volumes in this set provide information (name, address, telephone number, founding date, membership, staffing, divisions, publications, conventions and meetings) on national, nonprofit membership organizations in the United States. To locate anthropological-archaeological associations, refer to that category or use the alphabetical and key word index in volume 1.

Volume 2 provides a geographic and executive index. Volume 3 keeps the set up to date between editions by providing a list of newly reported associations and projects.

This publication is completely updated about every two years.

47. Bosch García, Carlos. *Guía de instituciones que cultivan la historia de América.* Mexico City: Instituto Panamericano de Geografía e Historia, 1949.

This is a listing of institutions throughout the world that are interested in the history of America. Arrangement is alphabetical by name of society, association, institution, or archive. Information per entry includes address, founding date, publications, membership requirements, and the extent of the library.

There is an index to countries and people but no specific subject index.

GRANTS AND RESEARCH CENTERS

There are a number of research centers, both in the U.S. and abroad, that have shown an interest in supporting archaeological research projects in Meso-America. Outstanding among these are the Wenner-Gren Foundation for

Anthropological Research, the New World Archaeological Foundation, the National Science Foundation, and the Mexican National Museum of Anthropology. To locate names of other such foundations in the United States, consult the *Research Centers Directory* and its supplement, *New Research Centers.* To locate research centers based in foreign countries, consult Sable's *Master Directory for Latin America,* the "Fourth International Directory of Anthropological Institutions" (45), or *World of Learning* (64). Haro (62) provides information on research centers in Canada and the United States, while McGlynn (2) lists research institutions in the United States, Middle America, and abroad.

The sizes of foundation grants vary from year to year. Information about grant support can be located in the *Annual Register of Grant Support,* which has a strong emphasis on United States foundations, and Thomas's *Grants Register, 1975-1977,* which has a more international flavor. For more current information, check recent issues of *Anthropology Newsletter* (38) or try searching the GRANTS data base.

48. Palmer, Archie M. *Research Centers Directory.* Detroit: Gale Research, ed. 1-, 1960-.

This biennial publication can be used to locate U.S. university-related research institutions and the independently operated, nonprofit organizations. Arrangement of the directory is by broad classification sections. Archaeology is listed under "Physical and Earth Sciences."

Information per listing includes such particulars as primary fields of research, special research facilities, media produced or distributed, periodical publications, conferences sponsored, source of support, annual research budget, and special library facilities.

Institutional and subject indexes are provided. Researchers will probably find that the easiest way to use this directory is to consult the subject index.

49. Sable, Martin H. *Master Directory for Latin America.* Los Angeles: Latin American Center of the University of California, 1965.

Although some of the information is out of date, this is still the most complete directory of its kind. A new edition will be invaluable.

This work, actually a compilation of ten directories, covers organizations, associations, institutions, and research centers throughout the world that are concerned with Latin America.

Arrangement is by type of institution. A subject index is provided.

50. *Annual Register of Grant Support.* Los Angeles: Marquis Academic Media, 1967-. Annual.

This standard reference work annually covers sources of non-repayable financial support. All types of foundations, from all areas of the world, are included. To locate foundations that offer grants for archaeological fieldwork, look in the subject index under "Archaeology." Information includes type of grant, eligibility requirements, number of applicants and awards, and application information. This book is also a good source of introductory material on grants (including how to write a grant proposal). A variety of indexes are provided.

51. Turner, Roland, ed. *Grants Register.* London: St. James Press, ed. 1-, 1969/70-.

Published biennially, this work covers various kinds of assistance available from government agencies and international, national, or private organizations. It includes scholarships, fellowships, research grants, exchange opportunities, vacation study awards, travel grants, grants-in-aid (for equipment, publishing, attending seminars, conferences, and courses), competitions, prizes, awards, and grants for a variety of artistic or scientific projects. Of the total of 2,146 awards listed, more than one-third are international in scope.

Two types of index are provided: a name index of awards and awarding bodies and a subject index, divided into sections for citizens or residents of specific countries as well as for nationals of all countries.

Arrangement of the main text is alphabetical by name of the organization. Information on each award includes the value, eligibility, frequency, number offered, closing date, etc.

This book also contains a bibliography of other sources of information, i.e., publications and useful foreign addresses.

52. GRANTS (data base). Santa Monica, California: System Development Corporation.

The GRANTS data base is currently offered for on line searching in the System Development Corporation's (SDC) ORBIT data management system. GRANTS corresponds to the Oryx Press's *Grant Information System.* The GRANTS data base has more than 1,500 listings of grant programs offered by federal, state, and local governments, commercial organizations, associations, and private foundations; the file is updated monthly. Users of this guide will be interested in the subject category "Archaeology."

INTERNATIONAL AGENCIES AND BODIES

Various international agencies and bodies take an interest in archaeological concerns. A listing of such organizations can be found in the *International Directory of Anthropological Institutions* (44), which, remember, is updated by the December 1967 issue of *Current Anthropology* (45) and, most recently, by McGlynn (2). Also keep in mind that Sable's *Master Directory* (49) lists international agencies and organizations that have shown an interest in Latin America.

Examples from such listings include organizations like the International Congress of Americanists; the United Nations Educational, Scientific, and Cultural Organization (UNESCO); and the Instituto Panamericano de Geografía e Historia. Examples of these organizations' publications can be found in the *International Directory of Anthropological Institutions* (44) and the *Current Anthropology* (45) update.

Unfortunately, bibliographies of these organizations' publications are difficult to locate and, when they exist, are usually incomplete. Following are a few examples of the kinds of bibliographies that might be found.

53. United Nations Educational, Scientific, and Cultural Organization. *Bibliography of Publications Issued by UNESCO or under Its Auspices: The First Twenty-five Years: 1946 to 1971.* Paris: UNESCO, 1973.

This is a classified bibliography of all works produced with UNESCO's help from 1946 to 1971. Users of this guide should be interested in sections 7 ("Protection of Monuments and Works of Art") and 8 ("Geography. Biography. History. Archaeology. Antiquities. Manuscripts.").

Examples of publications listed include those by Daniel Fernando Rubín de la Borbolla:

Guatemala: Monumentos históricos y arqueológicos, 1953.
Honduras: Monumentos históricos y arqueológicos, 1953.
México: Monumentos históricos y arqueológicos, 1953.

To bring this bibliography up to date, consult current issues of the *UNESCO List of Documents and Publications* (Paris: Computerized Documentation Serivce, 1951-).

54. Comas, Juan. *Los Congresos Internacionales de Americanistas: Síntesis histórica e índice bibliográfico general, 1875-1952.* Mexico City: Instituto Indigenista Interamericano, 1954.

Two-thirds of this work is devoted to a bibliography of the works published in the volumes of the International Congress of Americanists—more than 2,000 entries. The bibliography is classified and an author index is provided.

To update this work, consult:

_____. *Cien años de Congresos Internacionales de Americanistas: Ensayo histórico-crítico y bibliográfico.* Mexico City: Universidad Nacional de México, Instituto de Investigaciones Históricas e Instituto de Investigaciones Antropológicas, 1974.

This work has the same format as the 1954 bibliography.

GOVERNMENT AGENCIES

Government agency publications dealing with Mesoamerican anthropology are of two main types: those that cover site reports and those that cover antiquities laws. The two most important government agencies that issue these types of documents are the Instituto Nacional de Antropología e Historia in Mexico and the Smithsonian Institution in the United States. For a list of other government agencies, consult Sable's *Master Directory* (49). The *International Bibliography of Social and Cultural Anthropology* (11) provides an index to recently published government publications.

The Instituto Nacional de Antropología e Historia (INAH) in Mexico publishes a variety of documents relating to Mesoamerican archaeology.

INAH. *Anales.*
Boletín.
Guías. (These are guidebooks to various archaeological sites.)
Memorias.
Serie Investigaciones.

The antiquities laws in Mexico are both complex and strictly enforced. Before any archaeological work can be undertaken in Mexico, a permit must be obtained from INAH. Permission is granted only to professionals associated with reputable institutions. Two works, one of which was published by INAH, have been written covering the Mexican antiquities laws.

55. Instituto Nacional de Antropología e Historia. *Ley Orgánica del Instituto Nacional de Antropología e Historia,* 1963.

This document, written in Spanish, covers the general laws of INAH and the laws dealing with the protection and conservation of archaeological and historical monuments in Mexico. The articles of the law are spelled out, and appendices contain federal laws dealing with this topic.

56. Williams García, Jorge. *Protección jurídica de los bienes arqueológicos e históricos.* Xalapa, Veracruz: Universidad Veracruzana, 1967.

Williams García outlines the history of antiquities laws, quotes the laws, and provides interpretation and comments.

A bibliography is included.

For information on any changes in these laws that may have occurred since 1967, archaeologists may consult the following catalog of the United States Library of Congress, Hispanic Law Division:

57. U.S. Library of Congress. Hispanic Law Division. *Index to Latin American Legislation, 1950-60.* 2 vols.; 2 supplements. Boston: G. K. Hall, 1961.

The original volumes in this set cover the period 1950-1960. The supplements bring the coverage up to 1970.

This set provides a subject approach to legislation in Latin American countries. Arrangement is geographic by country. Within these divisions, the cards are arranged alphabetically by subject. Users of this guide will want to consult the heading "Cultural Property" under each Mesoamerican country.

For information on changes in the laws since 1970, contact INAH. Another work covers the antiquities laws of Guatemala.

58. Luján Muñoz, Luis. *Legislación protectora de los bienes culturales de Guatemala.* Guatemala: Instituto Antropología e Historia, 1974.

In the United States, a major government institution interested in archaeology is the Smithsonian Institution. The following book will lead users of this guide to a bibliography of the Smithsonian's publications in anthropology. For more recent information, check current issues of the *Monthly Catalog*[11] under "Smithsonian Institution" or order a data search from the Smithsonian Science Information Exchange (60).

59. United States. Smithsonian Institution. Office of Academic Programs. *Smithsonian Research Opportunities, 1969-1970.* Washington, D.C.: Government Printing Office, 1968. (Su. Doc. # 1.2:r31/1967-70).

This is a handbook and directory to the Smithsonian Institution's programs of study and research facilities. Arrangement is by grouping the programs under ten category headings. Users of this guide will want to turn to the "Anthropology and Cultural Studies" section to find information on the Smithsonian Office of Anthropology, its facilities, research staff, fieldwork, and publications. A major publication of this office is the *Smithsonian Contributions to Anthropology,* which began publication in 1965. It succeeds the *Bulletins* of the former Bureau of American Ethnology.

60. Smithsonian Science Information Exchange, Inc. (SSIE), Room 300, 1730 M.Street, N.W., Washington, D.C. 20036.

The SSIE is a nonprofit corporation of the Smithsonian Institution that offers a program for keeping abreast of new research in the social sciences by searching the SSIE data base. The Exchange collects information on and descriptions of research projects in progress. This information is made available even before the final reports are presented at meetings or in journals. The SSIE information is invaluable, as it identifies who is engaged in what research programs. This is important to researchers so that they may avoid duplication, identify leads to published literature, and learn about current research projects.

Users of this guide should be especially interested in the SSIE research packages in archaeology and anthropology (e.g., CV 02: Archaeological Excavations of New World Sites; CJ 12: Indians of North, Central, and South America: Characteristics, present conditions, services, anthropology, and history).

Contact SSIE for additional information.

SPECIAL LIBRARY COLLECTIONS

Numerous special collections exist for Latin American research and a few of these have strong collections in Mesoamerican archaeology. Usually the catalogs of these collections are photoduplicated and published in book form. Supplements keep the book catalog up to date.

Examples of special collections for which book catalogs are available are:

Harvard. *Catalogue of the Library of the Peabody Museum of Archaeology and Ethnology.*

Mexico City. *Catálogos de la Biblioteca Nacional de Antropología e Historia.*

Tulane. *Catalog of the Latin American Library,* University Library, New Orleans.

University of Texas Library, Austin. *Catalog of the Latin American Collection.*

Berlin. *Schlagwortkatalog des Ibero-Amerikanischen Instituts Preussischer Kulturbesitz in Berlin. Subject Catalog of the Ibero-American Institute in Berlin.*

When searching these catalogs, use standard LC subject headings.

To locate other special collections, consult:

Ash, Lee. *Subject Collections.* 1974.

Haro, Robert P. *Latin American Research in the United States and Canada.* 1971.

To locate special collections in Europe, check Lewanski's *Subject Collections in European Libraries. World of Learning* provides information on library and archival collections throughout the world, although no subject access is provided. Remember that both McGlynn (2) and Bosch García (47) provide a list of archives throughout the world that are interested in the history of America.

61. Ash, Lee. *Subject Collections.* 4th ed., revised and enlarged. New York: R. R. Bowker, 1974.

This is a subject guide to special book collections reported by university, college, public, and special libraries and museums in the United States and Canada. Users of this guide will wish to look at the following subject headings:

INDIANS OF NORTH AMERICA AND MEXICO
INDIANS OF CENTRAL AMERICA

Each entry under the subject headings is arranged geographically. Information under each listing includes the name and address of the collection, the number of volumes, and the informative notes.

62. Haro, Robert P. *Latin American Research in the United States and Canada: A Guide and Directory.* Chicago: American Library Association, 1971.

This publication provides access to two major sources of research: Latin American library collections and Latin American research centers. Only libraries and centers in the United States and Canada are included.

Arrangement is alphabetical by name of institution. For each,entry, subject strengths and directory-type information are provided. The subject index points to those institutions that have strong archaeological collections.

63. Lewanski, Richard C. *Subject Collections in European Libraries: A Directory and Bibliographical Guide.* New York: B.R. Bowker, 1965.

Lewanski's work may be used as a companion to Ash (61), as it covers special subject collections in Europe. Arrangement is by Dewey classification numbers. Refer to the 572-573 section, which covers the anthropological sciences. Arrangement within each section is alphabetical by country. Information is supplied for the number of volumes, the type of collection, who may use the facilities, etc.

A subject index to the classification scheme is supplied at the end of the volume.

64. *World of Learning.* 2 vols. London: Europa Publications, 1947-.

This work is important for its annual listings of academies, societies, research institutions, universities, libraries, archives, and museums. The work is arranged alphabetically by country. To locate a list of this sort, turn to the section for any country. An index of institutions is provided at the end of volume 2.

HUMAN RELATIONS AREA FILES

The Human Relations Area Files (HRAF) are a collection of primary source materials, including published books and articles, and some unpublished manuscripts, dealing with selected cultures and societies that represent all major areas of the world. These files, which are housed in selected libraries in the United States,[12] are intended primarily as data retrieval aids in doing cross-cultural studies. Two manuals, an *Outline of World Cultures (OWC)* and an *Outline of Cultural Materials (OCM),* provide access to information in the HRAF.

For more details, consult Robert O. Lagacé's *Nature and Use of the HRAF Files* (New Haven, Conn.: HRAF, Inc., 1974).

65. Murdock, George P. *Outline of World Cultures.* 5th ed. New Haven,

Conn.: HRAF, Inc. 1976.

This book is an index to the geographical culture areas represented in the Files. Use the index to locate specific Mesoamerican regions or culture groups.(e.g., Aztecs, Mayas, Tarascans). The index will direct the user to the unique code number (called the OWC code) for the culture group listed in the main body of this book; the main body provides specifics on what is covered in the Files for each culture group.

66. Murdock, George P. *Outline of Cultural Materials.* 4th revised ed. New Haven, Conn.: HRAF, Inc., 1961.

This manual is used to pinpoint subject categories of cultural materials. Use the index to locate subject areas of interest (e.g., archaeology, architecture, art) and refer to the main text for an explanation of what is covered by the subject heading.

By selecting a culture area from the *OWC* and a subject area from the *OCM*, a researcher can locate arcaheological, ethnographical, and ethnological specifics within and between cultures. For example, using HRAF it is quite easy to compare occurrences of cannibalism among the Aztecs with those from other culture groups throughout the world.

HRAF also makes available a variety of punched card data decks and a HRAFLIB Computer Program Library that includes several programs written in Fortran IV.

MUSEUMS

Museums of any size are important information centers for archaeologists. Often they not only house collections of artifacts but publish their own site reports and exhibit catalogs. Two of the larger museums with outstanding Mesoamerican archaeological collections are the Mexican National Museum of Anthropology in Mexico City and the Harvard Peabody Museum of Archaeology and Ethnology in Cambridge, Massachusetts.

In addition, in the Latin American countries there are hundreds of smaller museums housing special local and regional collections. Archaeologists must have some way of determining who has what. To that end, the following publications should be of value.

Hudson, Kenneth, and Nicholls, Ann, eds. *The Directory of World Museums.* 1975.

Clapp, Jane. *Museum Publications.* 1962.

Wasserman, Paul, ed. *Museum Media.* 1973.

Note also that McGlynn (2), the *International Directory of Anthropological Institutions* (44), the December 1967 issue of *Current Anthropology* (45), Ash's *Subject Collections* (61), *World of Learning* (64), and the *Guide to Departments of Anthropology* (76) all include some information on anthropological museums.

67. Hudson, Kenneth, and Nichols, Ann, eds. *The Directory of World Museums.* New York: Columbia University Press, 1975.

This is a directory of museums located around the world. Arrangement is alphabetical by country. Users should refer to the "Classified Index of Specialized and Outstanding Collections" section to locate the archaeology section. Under this section will be found a geographical listing of outstanding museum collections. Use this as an index and refer back to the main text to obtain information on areas of specialty, hours of operation, and addresses. Also check the section on anthropology.

Note: This book does not provide information on the museum curator's name, the founding date, or the museum's publications.

68. Clapp, Jane. *Museum Publications: A Classified List and Index of Books, Pamphlets and Other Monographs, and of Serial Reprints.* 2 vols. New York: Scarecrow Press, 1962.

Clapp's work is a classified bibliography of publications that are available for purchase from 276 museums in the United States and Canada. Included in the list are books, pamphlets, monographs, and serial reprints. For each publication listed, a code is given to identify the distributing museum.

Part one of this work covers anthropology, archaeology, and art; 4,416 publications are listed. Use the index ("Indians of Mexico, Central America and South America") to obtain numbers used in the main body. Pay careful attention to *See also* references. It is also possible to locate publications by referring to the Table of Contents, "Anthropology and Archaeology: Regional Anthropology: Indians of Mexico, Central and South America."

69. Wasserman, Paul, ed. *Museum Media: A Biennial Directory and Index of Publications and Audiovisuals Available from United States and Canadian*

Institutions. Detroit: Gale Research Company, ed. 1-, 1973-.

This work supplements and updates Clapp. It is a biennial directory of publications and audio-visual software available for purchase from institutions in the United States and Canada. Listing is by museum name; a title, key word, and subject index is provided. Use the subject index and locate the archaeology section for a list of museums that publish materials in this field, then refer back to the main text.

This book is more helpful for locating a list of the publications of a particular institution *if the institution's name is already known.*

ATLASES, MAPS, AND AERIAL PHOTOGRAPHS

Atlases and maps are indispensable to archaeologists. Maps may be published separately or as part of a magazine, journal, or book. Archaeologists must be able to locate site maps and obtain aerial photographs. The following sources should be of some assistance.

To locate archaeological site maps, users of this guide will wish to rely on the American Geographical Society's *Index to Maps in Books and Periodicals* and INAH's *Atlas arqueológico de la República Mexicana.* René Millon's *Urbanization at Teotihuacán* is an example of one of the more recently published field maps in Mesoamerican archaeology. Note also that most libraries contain worthwhile maps in their vertical files. Remember that Gropp (6) lists map bibliographies.

In addition to locating maps in libraries, archaeologists should try to build up their own map collections by obtaining maps issued by oil companies, government agencies, and magazine publishers. One excellent map showing Mesoamerican site locations with descriptive information was issued with the October 1968 issue of *National Geographic;*[13] this map has been available for purchase by members of the National Geographic Society.

70. American Geographical Society. Map Department. *Index to Maps in Books and Periodicals.* 12 vols. Boston: G. K. Hall, 1968; 1st supplement, 1971; 2nd supplement, 1976.

The basic set of this work consists of the photoduplication of 164,000 catalog cards of the map collection of the American Geographical Society. These volumes provide archaeologists with a way to find pertinent maps that have appeared in books and periodicals.

Entries are arranged alphabetically by subject and/or geographical-political division; arrangement within the division is chronological. To locate archaeological maps of Mesoamerica, use the following subject headings:

ARCHAEOLOGY–Name of Country
Name of Country–PRE-COLUMBIAN
AERIAL PHOTOGRAPHY–Name of Country

Two supplements bring this work up to 1976.

71. Instituto Nacional de Antropología e Historia. *Atlas arqueológico de la República Mexicana.* Mexico City: Instituto Panamericano de Geografía e Historia, 1939.

This book contains black and white fold-out maps showing the location of archaeological sites for each state in Mexico. Arrangement is alphabetical by name of state; under each state the sites are arranged alphabetically. Each site is pinpointed and described. Sample information includes the name of the site, the location of the nearest town, what has been discovered, how to get to the site, and a bibliographical reference if one exists.

For archaeological maps of Campeche and Quintana Roo, see: México. Departamento de Monumentos Prehispánicos. *Atlas arqueológico de la República Mexicana.* Mexico City: Instituto Nacional de Antropología e Historia, 1959.

72. Millon, René. *Urbanization at Teotihuacán, Mexico, Volume 1: The Teotihuacán Map.* Austin: University of Texas Press, 1973. 2 vols.

This publication is based on the results of a long-term project to prepare detailed archaeological maps of ancient Teotihuacán.

Part 1 of this set is entitled "The Text." It provides textual material on how to read the base map and its grid system; the field procedures used in the mapping project; architectural interpretations and hypothetical reconstructions of the archaeological map; observations and preliminary conclusions of the map and the survey; and photographs of the city.

Part 2 of this set, "Maps," consists of 147 map sheets (the field data), each with its own overlays (the interpretations of unexcavated structures discussed in Part 1). These map sheets and overlays are to be used in conjunction with the discussion of them in volume 1, part 1. Each map has been photogrammetrically constructed from aerial photographs.

Archaeologists interested in doing fieldwork will find the Pan American Union's *Index of Aerial Photographs* a useful source for locating published aerial photos. Since such photos need to be ordered by specifying exact geographical coordinates, the American Geographical Society's *Index to Maps of Hispanic America* may prove helpful. In addition, the United States Geological Survey's EROS Data Center at Sioux Falls, South Dakota[14] may be another useful source for obtaining aerial photographs. This center maintains files from four major sources: NASA LANDSAT Imagery and Data. NASA Manned Spacecraft Data, NASA Aerial Photography, and aerial photographs made over the past twenty-five years by various governmental agencies such as the departments of Agriculture and of Defense. Also, remember that the American Geographical Society's *Index to Maps in Books and Periodicals* (70) indexes aerial photographs.

73. Pan American Union. Department of Economic Affairs. *Indice anotado de los trabajos aerofotográficos y los mapas topográficos y de recursos naturales. Index of Aerial Photographic Coverage and Mapping of Topographic and Natural Resources.* Washington: Pan American Union, 1964-65.

This is a set of comprehensive map indexes covering published aerial photography, topographic and planimetric maps, geological maps, soil and vegetation maps. and land use and capability maps.

Each atlas in this series is devoted to a single country (for example, Number 6 covers Costa Rica, Number 9 covers El Salvador, Number 10 covers Guatemala, Number 12 covers Honduras, and Number 13 covers Mexico). The maps listed are ones generally available to researchers.

For each type of map, a map of the country is accompanied by a legend covering scale, date, institution responsible, and other descriptive information. Also included in the legend is a category entitled "Disponsibilidad," which provides researchers with information on how to locate the particular map.

For more information on how to use these indexes, read the introduction.

74. American Geographical Society. *Index to Maps of Hispanic America, 1:1,000,000. Washington: Government Printing Office*, 1943, 1944. 2 vols.

This is an index to the more than 200,000 geographical names on the

American Geographical Society's "Map of Hispanic America on the Scale of 1: 1,000,000" (commonly known as the Millionth Map). Arrangement is alphabetical by place name, and each place name is followed by the latitudinal and longitudinal coordinates. The names of physical features as well as towns are included.

Volume 1 of this set covers geographical names in Central America; volume 2 covers geographical names in Mexico. This index will be most useful to those who need to pinpoint geographical coordinates for ordering aerial photographs.

SPECIALISTS

At times, students of Mesoamerican archaeology may want to contact specialists in this field. Various sources may be used, among which are the *Fifth International Directory of Anthropologists,* the American Anthropological Association's *Guide to Departments of Anthropology,* and the *National Directory of Latin Americanists.* In addition, the *International Bibliography of Social and Cultural Anthropology* (11) includes in its "General" section a subdivision for "Biographies, Obituaries." The "General" section of the Royal Anthropological Institute's *Anthropology Index* (29) and the *Boletín bibliográfico de antropología americana* (13) also include biographical and obituary information. The June 1970 issue of *Current Anthropology*[15] contains a directory of anthropologists from around the world. McGlynn (2) provides a highly selective directory of individuals who have significantly contributed to Middle American anthropological research.

75. *Fifth International Directory of Anthropologists.* Chicago: University of Chicago Press, 1975.

This directory provides biographical information as well as research interests of almost 4,300 scholars in anthropology throughout the world. Arrangement is alphabetical by surname.

The various indexes—general, chronological (e.g., "Pre-Columbian"), subject or methodological (see "Section II: Archaeology"), and institutional—enable the user to identify Mesoamerican specialists.

76. American Anthropological Association. *Guide to Departments of Anthropology.* Washington, D.C.: American Anthropological Association, 1962-. Annual.

This is an annual directory of anthropologists working in academia or in museums. A rather new section includes directory information on research department personnel in the United States. For each of these types of anthropologists, arrangement is alphabetical by institution. Information is provided on both the institutions and the specialists.

This directory also lists, alphabetically by surname, those students who were recently granted Ph.D.'s in anthropology. The title and date of the dissertation are given.

Miscellaneous statistical information is appended.

Copies of this directory may be obtained from the American Anthropological Association.

77. United States. Library of Congress. Hispanic Foundation. *National Directory of Latin Americanists.* 2nd ed. Washington, D.C.: Library of Congress, 1971.

This work contains biographical information on 2,695 specialists who are permanent residents in the United States and who are involved in some type of Latin American academic discipline. Arrangement is alphabetical by surname.

For each specialist listed, the following information is included: name, birthdate, home and office address, major discipline, degrees received, professional career, honors, organization membership, research specialties and interests, publications, language knowledge, and linguistic studies.

An index to subject specialties is provided: use *both* "Anthropology" *and* "Archaeology."

ACADEMIC INSTITUTIONS AND FIELD SCHOOLS

Some sources for this type of information have already been discussed. They include the American Anthropological Association's *Guide to Departments of Anthropology* (76), the *International Directory of Anthropological Institutions* (44), and the December 1967 issue of *Current Anthropology* (45). Sable's *Master Directory* (49) also provides information on Latin American studies programs offered throughout the world. In addition, McGlynn (2) includes information on some academic institutions that sponsor activities in Mesoamerican anthropology. More generally, *World of Learning* (64) lists universities around the world along with their major faculty members.

For information on field schools, the Society for American Archaeology and the Archaeological Institute of America both publish lists of field schools to be held each year. Check the *Encyclopedia of Associations* (46) for these organizations' addresses. Other field school information can be found tacked on bulletin boards in university and college departments of anthropology. A further possibility is to contact the department's specialists. Information on current fieldwork can be found in the "Current Research" section of certain issues of *American Antiquity* (19) as well as in the *Boletín Bibliográfico de Antropología Americana* (13).

Information on academic institutions in the United States with Latin American studies programs can be found in Smith's *Directory of Latin American Studies Programs and Faculty in the United States.* Information on academic institutions based in Latin American countries can be found in Hilton's *The Scientific Institutions of Latin America.*

78. Smith, Margo L., compiler. *Directory of Latin American Studies Programs and Faculty in the United States.* Northeastern Illinois University: Consortium of Latin American Studies Programs, Publication no. 8, 1975.

This is a directory, compiled from the results of a 1973 questionnaire, of institutions in the United States that sponsor Latin American studies programs. The major portion of this publication is an alphabetical list of universities and colleges with descriptive information provided for each (degrees or certificates offered, faculty members, publications, special facilities and resources, financial aid, etc.).

In addition, several indexes are provided. These include an index of institutions listed by subject specialties (users of this guide will be interested in the "Anthropology" section), by those sponsoring field studies, and by location, as well as an index of Latin Americanist faculty members in the United States.

79. Hilton, Ronald. *The Scientific Institutions of Latin America, with Special Reference to Their Organization and Information Facilities.* Stanford, California: California Institute of International Studies, 1970.

This work focuses on scientific institutions and universities located in Latin American countries.

Arrangement is by country. A wealth of information is provided for each entry: background, publications, and size and important holdings of library collections.

BIOGRAPHICAL DICTIONARIES

Historical biographical dictionaries can help researchers obtain information on references to obscure historical figures. This is especially important for Mesoamerican researchers dealing with some of the lesser-known deities and historical persons in Mesoamerican history. To this end, García Granados's work proves a valuable sourcebook.

80. García Granados, Rafael. *Diccionario biográfico de historia antigua de Méjico.* Mexico City: Instituto de Historia, 1952.

The three volumes in this biographical dictionary cover ancient persons and mythical beings in Mexican history. Entries are arranged alphabetically and include the biographical source and page number of the information. Where applicable, the glyph symbol is also provided. Length of each entry varies according to the person's importance.

One-half of volume three is devoted to "Indios Cristianos de los Siglos XVI y XVII." The rest of the volume contains full bibliographic citations, indexes ("Indice Onomástico," "Indice de Jeroglíficos," "Indice Toponámico"), and dynastic charts.

NON-PRINT MATERIALS

General

Non-print materials for anthropology and archaeology include such audio-visual software as films, sound filmstrips, recordings, and slides and microforms. As might be remembered, the *Index to Literature on the American Indian* (12) includes a section on audio-visual materials, and Wasserman's *Museum Media* (69) incorporates sources of non-print materials into its listings. McGlynn (2) devotes a small section to non-book materials in the UCLA collection.

Other sources that may be used to locate titles and reviews of audio-visuals are Cox's *Hispanic American Periodicals Index* (28) and *American Anthropologist* (20), which devotes a part of each issue to a review of non-print materials.

The Library of Congress is another source that might be consulted. The *National Union Catalog*[16] periodically issues a volume on films and filmstrips that the Library has cataloged. Subject and title access is provided. The bibliographic information is fairly complete, but no attempt is made to provide any additional information.

Slides

Most archaeologists have established their own slide collections for various sites and artifacts. In addition, most major universities have slide collections that can be used by faculty members and authorized graduate students.

Another source of slides is the Archaeological Institute of America, which is attempting to develop a Slide Archive. The ultimate objective is to provide comprehensive, in-depth coverage of archaeological sites and materials from around the world. Interested persons may contact the Institute for additional information. The address is listed in the *Encyclopedia of Associations* (46).

Microforms

As the cost of publishing site reports becomes more and more prohibitive, archaeologists are turning to microforms. *Archives of Archaeology* represents a step in this direction. Published jointly by the Society for American Archaeology and the University of Wisconsin Press, *Archives of Archaeology* is a series of primary data sources on archaeological investigations related to the New Wor World. These reports, which include textual material as well as photographs and line drawings, are published on microcards and are available for purchase from the University of Wisconsin Press. A list of the publications available and purchasing information can be found in *American Antiquities*, 1969, volume 34, page 364. To see if a library already includes these microcards in its collection, look in the title portion of the library's catalog under "Archives of Archaeology." (Note: No new items have appeared in this series since 1971.)

SEARCH TECHNIQUES

The techniques of a literature search will vary according to the type of source being sought. In any case, the first step must always be a check of the library catalog (e.g., card catalog or on-line catalog) to see if the library has a particular work in its collection. Remember to use the subject headings listed earlier in this guide. If the work is not listed in the catalog, the next step will be to check in the *National Union Catalog.*[17] The *National Union Catalog* is a union list of all materials cataloged by the Library of Congress or by participating institutions. The approach is by author. The NUC will tell you which libraries have a copy of the particular work you are searching for. This is important for interlibrary loan purposes.

If you are trying to locate a serial publication, you will wish to consult the *Union List of Serials*[18] (for pre-1950 titles) or *New Serial Titles*[19] (for post-1950 titles). If you are interested in locating a copy of the serial within your own state, union lists are usually printed for each state (e.g., *Texas List*[20]). Since some Latin American periodicals may not be incorporated in the above-mentioned union lists, you may wish to consult the *Latin American Serial Documents* lists.

81. Mesa, Rosa Quintero, compiler. *Latin American Serial Documents: A Holding List: Volume 4: Mexico.* Ann Arbor: University Microfilms, Xerox Corp., 1970.

This volume is the fourth in a projected series of nineteen volumes providing researchers with information on holdings of Latin American serial publications in the United States and Canada. Arrangement is by title of publication. The entries include bibliographic information as well as who have which issues in their collection. Future volumes should cover other Mesoamerican countries.

Published proceedings of conferences can be located by various means. Some associations regularly publish papers presented at their conferences. In this case, check the library catalog under the name of the organization, looking for the title "Proceedings." However, many conference proceedings will not be covered by the library's catalog. For this reason, researchers should check in *Proceedings in Print* and/or in the *Directory of Published Proceedings.* McGlynn (2) details general information on organizations interested in Middle American anthropology that publish proceedings.

82. *Proceedings in Print.* Mattapan, Massachusetts: Proceedings in Print, v. 1, no. 1/2, October 1964-. Bimonthly.

Users of this guide will wish to refer to this publication beginning with volume 3, number 3 (from this volume forward the social sciences are covered). It is an index to conference proceedings that includes reports of conferences, lecture series, seminars, colloquia, symposia, congresses, hearings, and other meetings. Beginning with volume 3, number 3, all subject areas in all languages are covered.

Each volume in this series contains current entries (of proceedings published within the last two years) as well as retrospective entries. In each section, entries are arranged alphabetically according to the proceeding's own unique title and each entry is given a unique accession number.

For each entry, information is provided on the place, date, and sponsoring agency of the conference. When possible, ordering information is given.

Since the index of this series cumulates only annually, users will wish to refer to the subject index (located either at the back of each volume or bound separately). Use the subject headings "ARCHAEOLOGY" and "ANTHROPOLOGY." Under these headings will be found the title, date, and accession number for each proceeding indexed.

83. *Directory of Published Proceedings. Series SSH–Social Sciences/Humanities.* White Plains, New York: InterDok, v. 1, no. 1-, January 1968-. Quarterly.

The SSH series of this directory covers preprints and proceedings of congresses, conferences, meetings, symposia, and seminars held throughout the world. All areas of the social sciences and humanities are covered.

Arrangement is chronological by conference date, beginning from January 1, 1964. Each listing gives location and sponsor, as well as pertinent bibliographic information.

These volumes are indexed by author/editor, location, and subject/sponsor. Consult the subject/sponsor index for "Archaeology" and "Anthropology" and follow all *See* references. This index will provide the date and a code number; the next step is to locate that date in the main section and then find the citation code number under the date.

There are cumulative indexes that cover multiple volumes.

If you are interested in purchasing a particular work, consult *Books in Print,*[21] *Books in Series in the United States, 1968-1975,*[22] *Libros en Venta,*[23] or *Fichero Bibliográfico Hispanoamericano.*[24] If the work is not listed in one of these sources, it may be out of print. If so, you can check *Guide to Reprints*[25] or *Subject Guide to Microforms in Print*[26] to see if it has been reprinted.

Finally, one unique search technique method revolves around the *Social Sciences Citation Index.*

84. *Social Sciences Citation Index.* Philadelphia: Institute for Scientific Information, 1969-.

Various search avenues are available with this annual publication. These include the citation index, the corporate address index, the source index, and the permuterm subject index. At this time the work exhaustively covers 1,000 of the world's most important journals, including those in anthropology and archaeology. In addition, 2,000 other journals that contain important articles on the social sciences are covered selectively. Book reviews are noted in each of these indexes. For more information, read the introduction in the citation volume of this index.

Citation Index

This is an index devoted to authors who have been cited in recent periodical literature. Arrangement is alphabetical by cited author, then chronological by cited year. The reference contains the cited author's name, the reference year, and the name, volume, and page number of the publication. Under this are listed all the references to the source article that cited the particular author. By using this index, it is possible to find out who is being cited in the literature and who is doing the citing. A corporate author citation index is also included, which identifies which corporate bodies ahave recently been cited in the literature.

Corporate Address Index

This index gives a listing of all persons associated with a paritcular organization who have recently published materials in journals. For example, using this index it is easy to locate all faculty members from a particular institution who have recently published articles. Each listing gives the institution's address, the author's name, and references to where the article was published.

Source Index

This is a straightforward author index to the articles that are listed in the other components of the *SSCI*. Listings are alphabetical by author's surname. Complete bibliographical information is provided along with a list of references cited in the article. The author's address is also given.

Permuterm Subject Index

Designed as a type of subject index, this component of the *SSCI* lists permuted title words of journal articles. Since only significant title words are paired with one another, users will wish to consult such terms as "Archaeological,"

"Archaeology," "Mesoamerica," etc. Ample cross references are provided to help narrow the topic. Under each subject heading will be found a list of the names of all authors who have recently written on this subject. The next step is to consult the *Source Index* (above).

APPENDIX

LIBRARY OF CONGRESS CLASSIFICATION SCHEDULE
(Read down)

INDIANS OF MEXICO. ANTIQUITIES.

F 1219 General Works. Codexes.

Includes Montezuma I and II (but the Spanish Conquest = F 1230) and the ancient Acaxee, Aztecs, Chichimecs, Guachichile, Matlatzinca, Nahua, Olmecs, Otomí, Teco, Tepanecas, Tezcucan, Tlascalan, Toltecs, Totonacos, Zacateca, etc. For Mayas, see F 1435-1435.3. Modern tribes are classed in F 1221.

F 1219.1 Local (Ancient and modern), A-Z.

.C25 Campeche (State).
.C3 Casas Grandes.
.C35 Cerro de las mesas.
.C4 Chametla (Sinaloa).
.M5 Mexico City.
.M55 Michoacán (State). Includes Apatzingán (District).
.M6 Mitla. Officially: San Pablo Villa de Mitla.
.011 Oaxaca (State). Includes Monte Albán.
.Q5 Quintana Roo.
.T13 Tabasco (State). Includes La Venta.
.T24 Tenayuca San Bartolo (Pyramid).
.T43 Ticomán. Includes El Arbolillo.
.T7 Tres Zapotes.
.U8 Usumacinta Valley.
.V47 Veracruz (Vera Cruz) (State). Includes Isla de Sacrificios.
.Y8 Yucatán.

F 1219.3 Topics (Ancient and modern), A-Z.

.A5 Anthropometry.
.A6 Architecture.
.A7 Art.
.C2 Calendar. Chronology.
.C6 Commerce.
.C65 Cosmogony.
.C75 Costume.
.C8 Craniology.

F 1219.3.C9 Culture.
.D2 Dances.
.D9 Dwellings.
.E2 Economic conditions.
.L4 Law.
.M34 Magic.
.M4 Masks.
.M5 Medicine. Surgery.
.M52 Metalwork.
.M55 Military science.
.M58 Mines and Mining. Mineralogy.
.M59 Missions.
.M6 Monuments.
.N9 Numeral systems.
.P3 Paper and paper making.
.P5 Philosophy.
.P7 Politics and government.
.P8 Pottery.
.P84 Psychology.
.P9 Pyramids.
.R38 Religion and mythology.
.S5 Slavery.
.S6 Social life and customs.
.S7 Statistics.
.T3 Taxation.
.W6 Women.
.W65 Wood carving.
.W94 Writing. Picture writing.

Modern Indian Tribes. Ancient history of modern tribes is classed in F 1219.

F 1220 General works.

F 1221 Individual tribes, A-Z.
.A4 Akwa'ala.
.C3 Cahita.
.C38 Cazcan.
.C5 Chiapanec.
.C53 Chichimec Jonaz.
.C56 Chinantec.

F 1221 .C6 Cora.
.H8 Huastec.
.H85 Huave.
.H9 Huichol.
.K5 Kiliwa.
.L2 Lacandón.
.M3 Mayo.
.M35 Mazatec.
.M67 Mixe.
.M7 Mixtec.
.O6 Opata.
.O86 Otomí.
.P3 Pame.
.P6 Popoloca.
.S43 Seri.
.T25 Tarahumare.
.T3 Tarasco.
.T4 Tepehuane.
.T8 Tzeltal.
.T9 Tzotzil.
.Y3 Yaqui.
.Z3 Zapotec.
.Z6 Zoque.

INDIANS OF CENTRAL AMERICA. ANTIQUITIES. (Ancient and modern).

F 1434 General works.

F 1434.2 Topics (Ancient and modern), A-Z.
.A55 Anthropometry.
.M6 Missions.
.P8 Pottery.
.R3 Religion and mythology.

F 1434.3 Tribes (other than Mayas), A-Z.
Mayas.
Cf. F 1376, Yucatán.
F 1445, British Honduras.
F 1465, Guatemala.

F 1435 Mayas. General works.

F 1435 .A1-4 Periodicals. Societies.

F 1435.1 Mayas. Local, A-Z.

.B6 Bonampak.
.C47 Chan Kom.
.C5 Chichén Itzá.
.C63 Cogá.
.C7 Copan.
.H7 Holmul.
.K3 Kaminaljuyu.
.L2 Labná.
.P2 Palenque.
.P47 Petén.
.Q8 Quirigua.
.T5 Tikal.
.T8 Tulum.
.U2 Uaxactun.
.U7 Uxmal.
.X7 Xkichmook.
.Z3 Zaculeu.

F 1435.3 Mayas. Topics, A-Z.

.A6 Architecture.
.A7 Art.
.A8 Astrology.
.C14 Calendar. Chronology. Astronomy.
.F6 Folklore. Legends
.F7 Food.
.M3 Masks.
.M4 Medicine. Hygiene.
.N8 Numeration.
.P6 Picture writing.
.P8 Pottery.
.R3 Religion and mythology.
.S5 Sisal hemp.
.S7 Social life and customs.
.W6 Wood carving.

British Honduras. Belize (Belice). Antiquities. Indians (Ancient and Modern).

F 1445 General works.

F 1445 Including Mayas.
For Black Carib Indians, see F 1505.2.C3.

F 1445.1 Local, A-Z.
E.g., .S2 San Jose.

F 1445.3 Topics, A-Z.
E.G., .P6 Pottery.

Guatemala. Antiquities. Indians (Ancient and Modern).

F 1465 General works.
Including Mayas.
.P8 Popol vuh.

F 1465.1 Local, A-Z.
E.g., .P5 Piedras Negras.
.T3 Tajumulco.
.Z3 Zacualpa.

F 1465.2 Tribes, A-Z.
E.g., .C3 Cakchikel.
.C5 Chorti.
.J3 Jacalteca.
.K5 Kekchi.
Lacandón, see F 1221.L2.
.M3 Mam.
Pipil, see F 1485.2.P5.
.P6 Pokoman.
.Q5 Quichés.
.T9 Tzutuhil.
.X5 Xinca.

F 1465.3 Topics, A-Z.
E.g., .C8 Costume and adornment.
.F6 Folklore. Legends.
.R4 Religion and mythology.
.T4 Textiles.

Salvador (El Salvador). Antiquities. Indians (Ancient and Modern).

F 1485 General works.

F 1485.1 Local, A-Z.
E.g., .C8 Cuscatlán.

F 1485.2 Tribes, A-Z.
E.g., .P5 Matagalpa, See F 1525.2.M3.
Pipil.

F 1485.3 Topics, A-Z.
E.g., .P8 Pottery.

Honduras. Antiquities. Indians (Ancient and Modern).

F 1505 General works.

F 1505.1 Local, A-Z.
E.g., .T2 Tenampua.

F 1505.2 Tribes, A-Z.
E.g., .C3 Carib (Black).
.L4 Lenca.
Matagalpa, see F 1525.2.M3
Mosquito, see F 1529.M9.
.P3 Paya.
Sumo, see F 1525.2.S8.
.X5 Xicaque.

F 1505.3 Topics, A-Z.
E.g., .P6 Pottery.

Nicaragua. Antiquities. Indians (Ancient and Modern).

F 1525 General works.

F 1525.1 Local, A-Z.
E.g., .Z3 Zapatera Island.

F 1525.2 Tribes, A-Z.

E.g., Chiapanec, see F 1221.C5.
Lenca, see F 1505.2.L4.
Mosquito, see F 1529.M9.
.M3 Matagalpa.
.R3 Rama.
.S7 Subtiaba.
.S8 Sumo.
.T4 Terraba.
.U4 Ulva.

F 1525.3 Topics, A-Z.

E.g., .A7 Art.

Costa Rica. Antiquities. Indians (Ancient and Modern).

F 1545 General works.

F 1545.1 Local, A-Z.

E.g., .V6 Volcán Irazú.

F 1545.2 Tribes, A-Z.

E.g., .B6 Boruca.
.B7 Bribri.
Guaymi, see F 1565.2.G8.
.M3 Mangue.

F 1545.3 Topics, A-Z.

E.g., .A7 Art.
.P6 Pottery.

REFERENCES

1. Paul Kirchoff, "Mesoamerica," *Acta Americana* 1 (March 1943):92-107.

2. Hans Helfritz, *Mexican Cities of the Gods: An Archaeological Guide* (New York: Praeger, 1968), p. 9.

3. For example, Ralph L. Roys, trans., *The Book of Chilam Balam of Chumayel* (Washington: Carnegie Institution, 1933).

4. For example, *Popol Vuh: The Sacred Book of the Ancient Quiché Maya,* Eng. version by Delia Goetz and Sylvanus G. Morley, from the trans. of Adrián Recinos (Norman: University of Oklahoma Press, 1950).

5. For example, Bernal Díaz del Castillo, *The Conquest of New Spain,* trans. with an introduction by J. M. Cohen (Baltimore: Penguin Books, 1963).

6. *El Conquistador Anónimo: Relación de algunas cosas de la Nueva España y de la gran ciudad de Temestitán México. Escrito por un compañero de Hernán Cortés.* Ed. by León Díaz Cárdenas (Mexico City: Editorial América, 1941).

7. Fray Diego Durán, *Book of the Gods and Rites and The Ancient Calendar,* trans. and ed. by Fernando Horcasitas and Doris Heyden, with a foreword by Miguel León-Portilla (Norman: University of Oklahoma Press, 1921); idem, *The Aztecs: The History of the Indies of New Spain,* trans. by Doris Heyden and Fernando Horcasitas with an introduction by Ignacio Bernal (New York: Orion Press, 1964).

8. Fray Bartolomé de las Casas, *Apologética historia de las Indias,* ed. M. Serrano y Sanz (Madrid, 1909); idem, *Historia de las Indias,* 3 vols., ed. Gonzalo de Raparez (Madrid, 1927).

9. *Art Index* (New York: H. W. Wilson, v. 1-, 1929-).

10. The Center for Research Libraries is located in Chicago. Researchers wishing to request CRL materials must do so by going through the interlibrary loan office of their local library. Only member institutions enjoy borrowing privileges.

11. U. S. Superintendent of Documents, *Monthly Catalog of United States Government Publications* (Washington: Government Printing Office, 1895-, monthly).

12. *Behavior Science Research: The HRAF Journal of Comparative Studies* (New Haven: Human Relations Area Files, 1976).

13. "Archaeological Map of Middle America," *National Geographic,* October 1968.

14. U. S. Geological Survey, EROS Data Center, Garretson, Sioux Falls, South Dakota 57030.

15. "International Directory of Anthropologists: 1970 Revision," *Current Anthropology: A World Journal of the Sciences of Man* 11 (June 1970); "Associates in Current Anthropology" in the October-December 1971 issue of *Current Anthropology* adds to the preceding directory by publishing the names of those who were omitted in the June 1970 issue.

16. *National Union Catalog. Motion Pictures and Filmstrips, 1963-1967* (Ann Arbor: J. W. Edwards, 1969); *NUC. Motion Pictures and Filmstrips, 1968-1972* (Ann Arbor: Edwards, 1973); Library of Congress Catalogs, *Films and Other Materials for Projection, 1973* (Washington: Library of Congress, 1974); idem, *Films and Other Materials for Projection, 1974* (Washington: Library of Congress, 1975); idem, *Films and Other Materials for Projection, 1975* (Washington: Library of Congress, 1976); idem, *Films and Other Materials for Projection, 1976* (Washington: Library of Congress, 1977).

17. *National Union Catalog* (Washington: Library of Congress, 1956-); *National Union Catalog: Pre-1956 Imprints* (London: Mansell).

18. *Union List of Serials,* 3rd ed., 5 vols. (New York: Wilson, 1965).

19. *New Serial Titles: A Union List of Serials Commencing Publication after December 31, 1949: 1950-70 Cumulative,* 4 vols. (Washington: Library of Congress, and New York: Bowker, 1973); *New Serial Titles, 1971-1975 Cumulation,* 2 vols. (Washington: Library of Congress, 1976).

20. *Texas List* (Houston: Wilson Publishing Company).

21. *Books in Print* (New York: R. R. Bowker).

22. *Books in Series in the United States, 1965-1975* (New York: R. R. Bowker, 1977).

23. *Libros en venta en Hispanoamérica y España* (New York: Bowker, 1964); *Libros en venta en Hispanoamérica y España: Suplemento* (Buenos Aires: Bowker Editores Argentina, 1964-).

24. *Fichero bibliográfico hispanoamericano* (Buenos Aires: Bowker Editores, vol. 1-, October 1961-).

25. *Guide to Reprints, 1976* (Information Handling Services, Library Education Division, 1976).

26. *Subject Guide to Microforms in Print, 1962-1963* (Washington: National Cash Register, Microcard Editions, 1972).

ADDITIONAL REFERENCES

Adams, Richard E. W. *Prehistoric Mesoamerica.* Boston: Little, Brown, and Company, 1977.

Dumbarton Oaks Research Library and Collections, Center for Pre-Columbian Studies, *Studies in Pre-Columbian Art and Archaeology.* Washington, D.C.

Encyclopedia of World Art. 15 vols. New York: McGraw-Hill, 1968.

Hammond, Norman, ed. *Mesoamerican Archaeology: New Approaches.* Austin: University of Texas Press, 1974.

Kendall, Aubyn. *Art and Archaeology of Pre-Columbian Middle America: An Annotated Bibliography of Works in English.* Boston: G. K. Hall, 1977.

Landa, Diego de. *Relación de las Cosas de Yucatán, A Translation.* Trans. and edited by Alfred M. Tozzer. Papers of the Peabody Museum, vol. 18. Cambridge, Massachusetts: Peabody Museum, 1941.

Marquina, Ignacio. *Arquitectura prehispánica.* Mexico City: Instituto de Antropología e Historia, Secretaría de Educación Pública, 1951.

Maudslay, Alfred P. *Biologia centrali-americana,* vols. 58-63 of *Archaeology.* Text in vols. 58 and 63; plates in vols. 59-62. London: 1889-1902.

Rickards, Constantine G. *The Ruins of Mexico,* vol. 1. London: H. E. Shrimpton, 1910.

Sahagún, Fray Bernardino de. *General History of the Things of New Spain: Florentine Codex.* Trans. by Arthur J. O. Anderson and Charles E. Dibble. Santa Fe: School of American Research, 1950-.

Sanders, William T. and Price, Barbara J. *Mesoamerica: The Evolution of a Civilization.* New York: Random House, 1968.

Stephens, John L. *Incidents of Travel in Central America, Chiapas and Yucatán.* Illustrations by Frederick Catherwood. New York: Harper and Brothers, 1841; reprint ed., New York: Dover Publications, 1969.

Wauchope, Robert, ed. *Handbook of Middle American Indians.* 16 vols. Austin: University of Texas Press, 1964-.

Weaver, Muriel Porter. *The Aztecs, Maya, and Their Predecessors.* New York: Seminar Press, 1972.

Willey, Gordon R. *An Introduction to American Archaeology, Volume One: North and Middle America.* Englewood Cliffs, New Jersey: Prentice-Hall, 1966.

Index

Abstracts, 22
Abstracts of New World Archaeology (Woodbury), 22
Academic Institutions, 46
Aerial photographs, 42
American Anthropological Association, Guide to Departments, 45
American Anthropologist, 17
American Antiquity, 17
American Geographical Society, Index to Map of Hispanic America, 45
American Historical Association, Guide, 10
American Indian (Dockstader), 29
Anales (UNAM), *see* Comas, Indices generales de Anales de antropología, 21
Annual Register of Grant Support, 33
Annual Review (Siegel), 24
Anthropological Index to Current Periodicals (Royal Institute), 21
Anthropology Newsletter, 26
Antiquities laws, 35
Archives of Archaeology, 49
Architecture, 7
Art, 7
Ash, Subject Collections, 38
Associations, 29
Atlas arqueológico (INAH), 43
Atlases, 42
BBAA, *see* Boletín bibliográfico de antropología americana, 45
Bernal, Bibliografía de arqueología americana, 11
Bibliografía de arqueología (Bernal), 11
Bibliografía selectiva de las culturas indígenas de América (Comas), 12
Bibliographic Index, 13
Bibliographie Américaniste, 30
Bibliographies, Current, 12
Retrospective, 10
Bibliography of Latin American Bibliographies (Gropp), 10
Bibliography of Publications Issued by UNESCO, 34
Biennial Review (Siegel), 24
Biographical Dictionary, 48
Boletín bibliográfico de antropología americana, 45
Book Reviews, 24
Books in Print, 51
Books in Series, 51
Bosch García, Guía de instituciones, 31
Bulletin Signalétique, 22

Catalog of the Latin American Collection (University of Texas), 38
Catalog of the Latin American Library (Tulane), 38
Catálogos de la Biblioteca Nacional (Mexico City), 38
Catalogue of the Library of the Peabody (Harvard), 38

Center for Research Libraries, 27
Cien años de Congresos Internacionales de Americanistas; ensayo histórico-crítico y bibliográfico, (Comas), 35
Clapp, Museum Publications, 41
Columbus Memorial Library, *see* Pan American Union, Index to Latin American Periodical Literature, 19; Indice general de publicaciones periódicas, 19
Comas, Bibliografía selectiva de las culturas, 12; Cien años..., 35; Indices generales de Anales de antropología, 21; Los congresos..., 35
Comprehensive Dissertation Index, 27
Conference Proceedings, 50
Cox, Hispanic American Periodicals, 20
Current Anthropology, Fourth International Directory, 30; *see also* Yearbook of Anthropology, 29

Data base, *see* Smithsonian Science Information Exchange, 37
Data bases, *see* Comprehensive Dissertation Index (CDI), 27; Grants, 31; Hispanic Periodicals Index (HAPI), 20; Smithsonian Science Information Exchange, (SSIE), 37
Diccionario biográfico (García Granados), 48
Directory of Published Proceedings, 51
Directory of World Museums (Hudson), 40
Dissertation Abstracts International, 28
Dissertations, 27
Dockstader, American Indian, 29

Encyclopedia of Associations, 31
EROS Data Center, 44
Ethnohistory, 5

Field Archaeology, Journal of, 17
Field Schools, 46
Fifth International Directory of Anthropologists, 45
Fourth International Directory (Current Anthropology), 30

García, Carlos Bosch, *see* Bosch García, Guía de instituciones, 30
García, Jorge Williams, *see* Williams García, Protección jurídica de los bienes arqueológicos e históricos, 36
García Granados, Diccionario biográfico, 48
Government Agencies, 35
Granados, Rafael García, *see* García Granados, Diccionario..., 48
Grants (data base), 31
Grants Register (Turner), 33
Griffin, Latin America, 8
Grolling, *see* Tax and Grolling, Serial Publications, 16
Gropp, Bibliography of Latin American Bibliographies, 11
Guía a las reseñas (Matos), 25
Guía de instituciones... (Bosch García), 30
Guía de publicaciones (Levi), 14
Guide to Current Latin American Periodicals (Zimmerman), 14
Guide to Departments of Anthropology (AAA), 45
Guide to Historical Literature (American Historical Assoc.), 8
Guide to Reprints, 51
Guide to Reviews of Books (Matos), *see* Matos, Guía a las reseñas..., 25
Guides, 7

Handbook of Latin American Studies, 9

HAPI, *see* Hispanic Periodicals Index (Cox), 20
Haro, Latin American Research, 38
Harvard, Catalogue of the Library of the Peabody, 38
Harvard University Library, Latin America...Periodicals, 10
Hilton, Scientific Institutions of Latin America, 47
Hispanic American Periodicals (Cox), 20
HRAF, *see* Human Relations Area Files, 39
Hudson, Directory of World Museums, 40
Human Relations Area Files, 39
Humanities Index, *see* Social Sciences Index, 17

Ibero-American Institute (Berlin), Schlagwortkatalog des Ibero-Amerikanischen..., 38
INAH, *see* Instituto Nacional de Antropología e Historia, Atlas arqueológico, 43; Ley orgánica, 35
Index of Aerial Photographic Coverage, *see* Indice anotado de... aerofotográficos..., 44
Index to Latin American Legislation (Library of Congress), 36
Index to Latin American Periodical Literature (Pan American Union), 17
Index to Latin American Periodicals, *see* Indice general de publicaciones periódicas..., 17
Index to Literature on the American Indian, 13
Index to Maps (American Geographical Society), 44
Index to Map of Hispanic America (American Geographical Society), 45
Indice anotado de...aerofotográficos... (Pan American Union), 44
Indice general de publicaciones periódicas, 17
Indices generales de Anales... (Comas), 21
Instituto Nacional de Antropología e Historia, Atlas arqueológico, 43; Ley orgánica, 35
International Agencies, 34
International Bibliography of Social and Cultural Anthropology, 13
International Bibliography of the Social Sciences, *see* International Bibliography of Social..., 13
International Directory...(Thomas), 30
International Directory of Anthropologists, *see* Fifth International Directory, 45
International Index, *see* Social Sciences Index, 18
Irregular Serials and Annuals, 15

Journal de la Société des Americanistes, 17
Journal of Field Archaeology, 17
Journals, 17

Katunob, 17

Lagacé, Nature and Use of HRAF, 39
Latin America: A Guide (Griffin), 9
Latin America and Latin American Periodicals (Harvard), 12
Latin American Serial Documents (Mesa), 50
Latin American Research (Haro), 38
Legislación Protectora (Luján Muñoz), 36
Levi, Guía de publicaciones, 14
Lewanski, Subject Collection in European Libraries, 39
Ley orgánica (INAH), 35
Libraries, *see* Special Library Collections,37

Library of Congress, *see* U.S. Library of Congress, Index to Latin American Legislation, 36; National Directory of Latin Americanists, 46
Libros en venta, 51
Los Congresos... (Comas), 35
Luján Muñoz, Legislación Protectora, 36

Maps, 42
Master Directory (Sable), 32
Matos, Guía a las reseñas, 25
McGlynn, Middle American Anthropology, 8
Mesa, Rosa Quintero, Latin American Serial Documents, 50
Mexico City, Catálogos de la Biblioteca Nacional, 38
Microforms, 49
Middle American Anthropology (McGlynn), 8
Millón, Urbanization at Teotihuacán, 43
Millionth Map, *see* Index to Map of Hispanic America (American Geographical Society), 45
Murdock, Outline of Cultural Materials, 40; Outline of World Cultures, 39
Museum Media (Wasserman), 41
Museum Publications (Clapp), 41
Museums, 40

NASA, *see* EROS Data Center, 44
National Directory of Latin Americanists (Library of Congress), 46
National Union Catalog, 48
Nature and Use of HRAF (Lagacé), 39
New Research Centers, 31
New Serial Titles, 49
New York Times Index, 26
Newsforms, 25
Nicholls, *see* Hudson and Nicholls, Directory of World Museums, 40
NUC, *see* National Union Catalog, 48

Outline of Cultural Materials (Murdock), 40
Outline of World Cultures (Murdock), 39

Palmer, Research Centers, 32
Pan American Union, Index to Latin American Periodical..., 17; Indice general de publicaciones periódicas, 17
Pan American Union, Indice anotado de...aerofotográficos..., 44
Peabody Museum, *see* Harvard, Catalogue of the Library of the Peabody, 38
Periodicals, Directories, 14; Indexes, 17; Sample, 15
Pikelis, *see* Thomas and Pikelis, International Directory, 30
Proceedings, 50
Proceedings in Print, 50
Protección jurídica (Williams García), 36

Quintero Mesa, *see* Mesa, Rosa Quintero, 50

Research Centers, 31
Research Centers (Palmer), 32
Reviews, 24
Revista mexicana de estudios antropológicos, 30
Royal Anthropological Institute, Anthropological Index, 21

Sable, Master Directory, 32
Schlagwortkatalog des Ibero-Amerikanischen..., 38
Scientific Institutions of Latin America (Hilton), 47
Search Techniques, 49
Serial Publications in Anthropology (Tax), 16

Siegel, Annual Review, 28; Biennial Review, 24
Slide Archives, 49
Slides, 49
Smith, Directory of Latin American Studies Programs, 47
Smithsonian Institution, Smithsonian Research, 37
Smithsonian Research... (Smithsonian Institution), 37
Smithsonian Science Information Exchange Data Base, 37
Social Sciences Citation Index, 51
Social Sciences Index, 17
Société des Americanistes, Journal, 17
Societies, 29
Sources of Information in the Social Sciences (White), 8
Special Library Collections, 37
Specialists, 45
SSIE, *see* Smithsonian Science Information Exchange, 37
Standard Directory of Newsletters, 26
Subject Collections (Ash), 38
Subject Collections in European Libraries (Lewanski), 39
Subject Guide to Microforms in Print, 51

Tax, Serial Publications, 16
Texas List, 50
Theses, 27
Thomas, International Directory ..., 30
Transactions of the American Philosophical Society, 30
Tulane, Catalog of the Latin American Library, 38
Turner, Grants Register, 33

Ulrich's International Periodicals Directory, 15
UNAM, Anales, *see* Comas, Indices generales de Anales, 21
UNESCO, *see* United Nations Educational, Scientific, and Cultural Organization, Bibliography
Union List of Serials, 49
United Nations Educational, Scientific, and Cultural Organization, Bibliography..., 34
Universities, 46
University of Texas, Catalog of the Latin American Collection, 38
Urbanization at Teotihuacán (Millón), 43
U. S. Library of Congress, Index to Latin American Legislation, 36; National Directory of Latin Americanists, 46

Wasserman, Museum Media, 41
White, Sources of Information..., 8
Widener Library Shelflist, *see* Harvard University Library, Latin America ...Periodicals, 10
Williams García, Protección jurídica, 36
Woodbury, Abstracts of New World Archaeology, 22
World of Learning, 39

Yearbook of Anthropology, 29

Zimmerman, Guide to Current Latin American Periodicals, 14